Advance Praise for GROUNDED

"Moving... Courageous... Deeply personal."

Martin Sheen
Actor, Co-Author (with Emilio Estevez) of
"Along The Way, The Journey of a Father and Son"
Malibu, California

"Kendall's compelling story has been grafted into the narrative God has written with his one Word, his Son Jesus. Kendall freely witnesses to the heavenly Father's saving mercy as Christ asks all earthly fathers and sons, mothers and daughters, to do. This intrepid former pilot calls things by name, opens himself to conversion, and humbly suffers whatever it takes to be as present as possible to those God has entrusted to him. When God's proposal is accepted as Mary and Joseph—and Kendall—have done in their own personal way, then we can hope that others will be able to locate their own stories within God's saving plan for all humanity."

William M. Joensen
Bishop, Diocese of Des Moines (Iowa)

"Ken has been through a major life-changing event that has challenged his Catholic Faith and would challenge anyone's Faith. His ability to give control of his life over to the Trinity and his Catholic Faith is a blessing and a lesson to be learned by all. We are not the controllers of our Universe, no matter how smart we think we are. I truly believe those that read the book will have a filling of the Holy Spirit and a life-changing conversion in their faith and relationship to the Trinity."

Richard Harmon
Grand Knight, St. Elizabeth Seton Council of the Knights
Carlisle, Iowa

"We shall not cease from exploration,

And the end of all our exploring

Will be to arrive where we started

And know the place for the first time."

T. S. Eliot

GROUNDED

A Different Kind of War

Kendall P. Geneser

Concordis
Publishing

CONCORDIS
PUBLISHING

501 South Market Street
Oskaloosa, IA 52577
concordispublishing.com

First Concordis Publishing Softcover edition March 2022

For information about special discounts for libraries, charitable organizations, or bulk purchases, please contact Concordis Publishing Special Sales at 1-310-650-0213.

DESIGNED BY RODNEY V. EARLE

Manufactured in the United States of America

10 9 8 7 6 5 4 3 2 1

Library of Congress Cataloging-in-Publishing Data Pending

ISBN: 978-0-578-31171-5 (Softcover)
ISBN: 978-0-578-31172-2 (eBook)

Contents

"And he said unto me, My grace is sufficient for thee; for My strength is made perfect in weakness." 2 Corinthians 12:9

A Different Kind of War

Kendall P. Geneser

Dedication

To all those that helped me—in every way—get to this place in my life. To my wife, our boys, and my entire family. To my friends and neighbors who travel with me on this little spinning rock. None of us know for sure how or where our journey will end. I only know that getting there would have been impossible without every one of you. This story is possible only because of the people in my life. Thank you.

Best wishes

&

God Bless

Kendall Hansen

Foreword

More than a decade has slipped away since I promised that I would update readers with a sequel to *The Gift*, my novella-sized memoir detailing the trials and travails of living with Multiple Sclerosis. This work is that long-awaited sequel, sort of.

The reality is that with the passage of time, I believe my perspective is broader and, more importantly, more profound. While I do not fancy myself a religious scholar—I am just an average dude—I do think my message is so blatantly obvious that even I can share its wisdom.

This work goes far beyond my struggles. We all have our "crosses to bear," and this work is simply the story of how I choose to bear mine. Maybe it can help you find inspiration for bearing your own.

> "When seventy years are completed for Babylon, I will visit you, and I will fulfill to you my promise and bring you back to this place. For I know the plans I have for you, says the LORD, plans for welfare and not for evil, to give you a future and a hope. Then you will call upon me and come and pray to me, and I will hear you. You will seek me and find me: when you seek me with all your heart, I will be found by you, says the LORD, and I will restore your fortunes and gather you from all the nations and all the places where I have driven you, says the LORD, and I will bring you back to the place from which I sent you into exile." Jeremiah 29: 1-14

Preface

> "I went to the woods because I wanted to live deliberately... I wanted to live deep and suck out all the marrow of life... to put aside all that was not life, and not, when it came time to die, discover that I had not lived."
>
> *Henry David Thoreau*

This is the story of how I have found life. Found it in all its wonderful abundance.

"I AM MORE ALIVE TODAY THAN I HAVE EVER BEEN."

The long and winding path of physical being continues. Though I do not rightly know what is around the next bend, I will keep forging ahead. That is because I know where it ends.

Introduction

"If God seems slow in responding, it is because He is preparing a better gift. He will not deny us. God withholds what you are not yet ready for. He wants you to have a lively desire for His greatest gifts. All of which is to say, pray always and do not lose heart."

Saint Augustine

In retrospect, Saint Augustine's sentiments look to be spot on. *Grounded: A Different Kind of War* was originally intended as a long-promised update to *The Gift.*

Through serious introspection, I have managed to uncover the hidden gem, the fine pearl of life. Information that you, the reader, will hopefully consider vital to understanding this work and what is important for your own brief existence on this lonely planet.

As for me, my life is much different than the path I had envisioned. But I choose to believe that God has given me a different kind of war to fight. I think the path I am on now, with my willing cooperation, is the one true path. It is the path that will bring me home.

Chapter One:

Guadalcanal

Hot lead streamed from my fifty-caliber gun as I fired at the Zero bearing down on our bomber. My compatriot, Marty, and I stood back to back and fought for our lives while our airplane droned mindlessly toward its target, a speck of green in an endless sea. Suddenly, the plane lurched sideways, nearly knocking us off our feet. Like a pack of hungry wolves, the tiny zeroes swarmed. "GUADALCANAL!" Marty screamed as he fired. Coms were down, so I made my way to the front to check on the rest of the crew. They were all gone. I pulled the co-pilot's body out from behind the controls and suddenly found myself piloting the warbird toward our target. The cockpit smelled like freshly cut hay.

"Time for supper," my sister screamed above the wind whistling through the bullet holes in our windscreen.

"Marty's mom says it's time for him to go home, too," she yelled.

"What are we havin'?" I asked as I climbed out of our horse trailer, the imaginary bomber from which my next-door neighbor, Marty, and I had fought many a battle.

"I think spaghetti," she said as I brushed the hay of our imaginary cockpit from my jeans.

The glamour of war, that knife in your teeth, silk scarf flapping in the breeze mystique had already managed to permeate every fiber of my being. Although we were just playing war, I knew that someday I would be a knight of the sky, an airborne warrior. I wanted to fly, and not only from point A to B. I wanted to fight in the sky.

No story is completely clean if it is true. Reality is messy. I cannot honestly tell you that I achieved my goals because of my laser focus or that my path remotely resembled a straight line. I will say that despite the many twists and turns of life, in my early years, there was always the invisible pull of the sky. To this day, if I hear an airplane traversing the heavens above, I cannot help but look up.

When I was six, my mom bought me a toy instrument panel. It was a little plastic thing with a single yoke that you could turn and push in and pull out. The attitude indicator would move as you turned the yoke. My mom had taken flight lessons at some point before motherhood, and we spent hours flying at the kitchen table, my little plastic cockpit getting a rest only at mealtime. Years later, the kitchen table was the place where she and I would spend hours building model airplanes.

When I was seven, Dad talked a man into giving us a ride in his airplane. Dad does not like flying. He considers it an unnatural means of transport, but he climbed into the little airplane's back seat that day and accompanied my sister and me once around the pattern. I suppose he figured it would be better to die in a fiery crash than to have to face our mother and explain that both her children had expired. That trip, less than a five-minute circuit around a farmer's field, was the first time I ever flew.

Yet, life's journey is a long and winding road. Only weeks after my first flight, life interjected a significant detour. I went from the sandbox to the sandlot. My little hometown got little league baseball. The problem was that because the town was so small, the eight-year-old team that they were trying to form only had eight people sign up. At seven, I was essentially drafted to play with the eight-year-old kids. I considered it a great honor to play with the big kids.

As the only seven-year-old on the eight-year-old team, I spent most of the season in the outfield. That said, even though I was seven, I wasn't the worst player on the team. Thus, I played left field instead of right.

In those days, very few of the teams we faced could even hit the ball out of the infield. I'd only had one fly ball hit to me all season. I caught it, but I spent every inning hoping no one would hit the ball out to me.

As recounted in *The Gift*, it was the last game of the season when the second fly ball of the year came my way. It was a towering fly ball but rather shallow. It had rained that day. As such, the grass was still wet. In those days, cleats for kids were cheap plastic and, consequently, very slick when wet. At some point, as I sprinted in to catch the fly ball, I realized that it was carrying farther than I had initially judged. I slammed on the brakes and almost instantly found myself sliding flat on my back. I remember the disappointment and shame that I felt as I slid feet first toward shortstop.

I'm a failure. The big kids are going to hate me. Then I remembered the fly ball aloft somewhere and glanced into the skies above. The ball was about to rendezvous with my face. I thrust my hands toward the heavens, closed my eyes, and turned my head. The ball landed squarely in my mitt. That happy accident instantly brought me into the limelight. I liked it. Over the years, I've honed this "aw shucks, nothin' to see here" persona that masked delusions of grandeur. Of course, today, I know that growing up, I was simply a decent-sized fish in a tiny pond. Back then, my dream of flying took a back seat to baseball.

Thus began an odyssey that I chased for the next fifteen years of my life. Looking back, it seems a wasted decade and a half, but the reality is that the time I spent as an athlete informed the way I think, the way I strive to act, and my attitude toward life. People decry our nation's fascination with athletics, and indeed, in many ways, their arguments are valid. Yet, I would simply point out that my grit and determination, things I still use every day of my life, are not the product of any classroom. They are the product of the fields and courts of my youth.

For many years I chased the dream of playing baseball professionally. In retrospect, this was a ridiculous notion. I became a decent pitcher. I'm a lefty and in little league, and, in some ways, all the way through high school, this proved an advantage. In those days, in the tiny bergs where I played, left-handed pitching was an oddity. In my delusional state, I mistook my early success for talent. I was—by the time I finished high school—enjoying great success. Local fans started to believe that our team could win against anyone if I were pitching. I, too, began to believe the hype.

The cold hard truth was slow in revealing what it had always known. I was twenty-one years old when I finally realized that my physical tools were sorely lacking.

In my immediate family, there were no college graduates. Me going to college was simply the next logical step on my journey to the major leagues. I chased this dream with reckless abandon until the summer after my junior year in college. A friend and mentor—my boss at Mickey Owen Baseball School, where I had spent many summers since I was eleven—finally suggested that I should pursue a career in coaching. "Those who can, do. Those who can't..." This rather obvious revelation summarily crushed me. It was the first obstacle in my seemingly charmed life.

My friend and mentor—also a left-handed pitcher—had played the game at its highest level. He probably knew the very first time that he saw me throw that I had a snowball's chance in hell of making it to "the show." Now he was trying to let me down easily. I thought he had invested endless hours teaching me how to be a better pitcher—he had. Yet his most important lesson was teaching me how to be a better man.

Chapter Two: Reality

I suppose my cocksure ignorance—delusional at best—was fueled by my parents. My dad always told me, "be a leader, not a follower." He hoped that I would not succumb to the peer pressure of drugs or alcohol. It worked, at least through high school. Maybe too well. Not only did I avoid the pitfalls of vice, but I also had this obsessive compulsion to lead.

Yet this sickness masks a mostly undetected tendency to favor sloth and apathy. It boils down to the notion that I felt privileged. On the surface, a carefully crafted persona of false modesty harbored a deep-seated level of confidence born out of a tendency to win, lead, and be number one. I was never a world-beater of true greatness. I only stood out among my peers in my immediate surroundings. That's because underlying it all, sloth and apathy were the foundation of my faulty tower. I didn't want to be good. I just wanted to be good enough. The result is that I grew up believing I was a little better than I was. The reality was that I was only swimming in a small tributary of a much larger body of water. In that shelter, I grew and flourished, confident that one day I'd stand on the hill at Yankee Stadium in the fall.

What's the saying? "If you want to hear God laugh, tell him your plan." I didn't realize it, but when I was seven, I'd just started the ultimate "Guy walks into a bar" joke for the big guy. The punchline would take nearly half a century, and the joke would be on me.

Despite the crushing disappointment and a perceived necessity to find that "next big thing" in my life, great good had come from my baseball chase. In undergraduate school, I played baseball, but more importantly, I learned how to learn. I developed an inquisitive mind and began to venture out of the tiny tributary that had been my refuge.

As mentioned, I wasn't good. I'd discovered that at a Reds tryout one summer in late July. They kept me for the scrimmage that followed the tryout, and I faced a guy throwing ninety-three miles per hour. I was a junior in college, but I was playing NCAA Division III, and the best fastball I'd ever seen was eighty-seven. The guy walked me on four pitches. Yet, it only required one pitch to realize that I had no business there. I could have carried an axe or a shovel or maybe a toothpick to the plate that day. Despite wielding my favorite bat, my hitting the ball was an absolute physical impossibility. A pitcher throwing eighty-seven, I had a shot, ninety-three, no chance. That tryout was roughly concurrent with the shocking news that my dream was just that, a dream.

That double whammy delivered in relatively quick succession was a one-two combo that left me reeling. This sudden, perceived vacuum in my life's mission found me scrambling for purpose and meaning.

As a junior in college, about to begin my senior year, the shifting of gears was not nearly as dramatic as it seemed. Recall that college had broadened my horizon. I was working toward a double major in Economics and Business Management with a minor in coaching. I was intrigued by matters of business, economics, and finance. As a freshman, I was a devout Democrat. I'd developed, and in some respects still retain, a penchant for American history and politics. I had honed an unhealthy obsession for JFK and all things Camelot. I devoured every book that he was purported to have read or written. I was particularly interested in the story of our slain president, so young, so vibrant, so full of the promise of what could be, what almost was. I was still hovering somewhere between an infant and a toddler in November of sixty-three, but the legend of Camelot would have a far-reaching impact on my life.

While I devoured "Talleyrand" or "Pilgrim's Way" by day, I learned about the Laffer Curve or the Marginal Propensity to Consume. I'd grown up in a town full of FDR. Democrats. Yet, slowly, my eyes were opening to the fallacy of liberal thinking.

In terms of my socio-economic background, I grew up in the lower to the mid-level middle class. My favorite professor told us in a lecture once that one of the most challenging and unlikely scenarios in life is to transcend one's socio-economic status. I remember feeling many things, such as momentary surprise, disappointment, and then a mild resistance to this statement. Ted Turner once said that "money was simply a way of keeping score." I had developed a somewhat competitive mindset by then. Mr. Turner's assertion sounded right.

My favorite professor was a cross between Hal Holbrook and Jimmy Stewart, with a touch of Sir Paul McCartney thrown in. I heard my first lecture from him when I was a freshman. It was a profound experience. It was an entertaining performance rivaling any speech, any homily, or any monologue that I'd ever heard. Yet this performance was packed with academic knowledge. Unlike me, he never phoned it in. I would have the privilege to listen to many of his lectures over the next four years, but after the first, I knew. I declared my major that day. During my time at William Penn, I developed the ability to think critically. I became wholly immersed in academia and the pursuit of knowledge. Well, up to a point.

Education was important, but my real reason for being there was so a scout could come to draft me. As a freshman, while my real purpose was to further my baseball career, I soon discovered that academia was refreshing. It made me think about things differently. As mentioned, no one in my immediate family had experienced post-secondary education. I was the first. In some respects, this was scary. I was afraid to fail. That fear propelled me to great success. I ended the fall semester with a grade point average of 3.875. In my pea-sized brain, I had it all figured out.

Chapter Three:
Wayward Son

College is a place to explore, a place to experiment, a place to stretch and grow, and a place to fly and be free. With freedom, however, one should employ equal measures of responsibility, maturity, and discretion. I say this after more than half a century of walking on this planet. At age nineteen, I was a train wreck.

I joined a fraternity. It was not the preppy kind. It was like Animal House on steroids. My God, it was fun. God? Alas, my maker seemed far away. The level of my debauchery resulted in a plummeting grade point average. I was not an alcoholic, but I became a serious binge drinker.

I pledged my fraternity in the spring of nineteen eighty-two. Spring is the heart of the college baseball season. We were on back-to-back road trips. I was also in the throes of one of the most challenging classes in my chosen major, Macroeconomics. It was a monumentally busy time. It was the busiest I'd seen in all my nineteen years. I left for a baseball trip just days before a major paper was due in Macro. I had not yet started that paper.

On the bus, I was "reading" a copy of *Playboy* and ran across an article on ways the U.S. might use currency manipulation to effect certain desired outcomes with its trading partners in Latin America. It was macroeconomics and expounded quite eloquently on economic theories that I'd danced around for weeks. It wasn't the first time that I'd been impressed by the literary content, not just the glossy pictures in the magazine. It was the answer to all my prayers. Mere hours before it was due, I made a monumentally stupid decision. I plagiarized. Remember me mentioning that my professor never phoned it in? Without a doubt, this remains the best example of me phoning it in—taking a shortcut—of my entire life.

However, I spent the rest of the week thinking I was a hero. I was wondering if my paper would come back with an A or an A+.

We got back from another road trip on Sunday. I spent a few hours getting hazed by my future fraternity brothers. Monday morning, we got our papers back. I was shocked and instantly sweating when I opened my paper to see "F. See me after class." As per normal, my favorite professor delivered his usual virtuoso performance. Sadly, I don't remember a word. That said, I don't believe I'll live long enough to forget his next speech.

After class, I walked down the hallway like it was the "green mile." My professor was only a few feet ahead of me. He unlocked his office door and went inside. He sat down at his desk and reached wordlessly for my paper. I closed the door and then handed it over.

His office was a cliché of the typical college professor's workplace. Bookcases filled to the brim were on three of the walls surrounding the desk. There were papers stacked neatly on the corner of the desk. Behind him, a single window ran from floor to ceiling.

"You know, I read *Playboy*, too," he said.

"Professor, I—"

He stopped me cold, raising his hand like a traffic cop. "Look, I know you're really busy right now. I get it. But this is the kind of thing people go to prison for. This isn't you just cheating on a paper, violating the school's moral code. This is essentially a crime."

"I know. I—"

This time, he stopped my would-be diatribe with a look. "You know, a lot of people think President Nixon was just caught up in the circumstances of Watergate and that he was just trying to cover up an embarrassing situation. But you know what I think. I think he was a crook. He got away with so much for so long, and he probably started by plagiarizing a term paper."

The disappointment on his face was palpable, and I'm sure mine was even worse. I wanted to say something to justify my deplorable behavior, but my voice was now conspicuously absent.

"I'm sorry," I finally said. "It was wrong. It was a shortcut I should not have taken."

"There's an understatement. You write well. Your grasp of the subject matter thus far seems solid. Why, suddenly, did you feel the need to cheat?"

"There are so many demands on my time. I guess I just tried to take the easy way out."

"The question is, are you sorry, or just sorry you got caught?"

Truth be told, it was probably more the latter. Looking back, though, that pivotal moment, that life path correction, rendered by a man in whom I thought the sun rose and set, was the first of many such corrections in my life.

Given my relative success in the class thus far, an F on the paper would reduce my grade to C. If I completed the assigned extra credit, my grade would be a B minus. I would have the opportunity to rewrite the paper I had plagiarized, and whatever grade I got would be lowered by one full letter grade for being late. If I got an A on the final, it was conceivable that I could still get an A in the class.

I vaguely recall stumbling down the middle of a snowy street in an early spring blizzard going... God only knows where but proceeding in great haste. When a young lady pulled alongside, rolled her window down, and asked, "Where the hell are you going?"

"Dunno. I think I was headin' over to your place." I smiled.

"You're a drunken idiot. You're acting like an asshole," my future wife scolded. "Get in."

My tailspin into this morass of debauchery was sudden and severe. My GPA plummeted from 3.875 to 2.9. Yet this foray into the lunacy of moral relativism was not totally devoid of grace. As utterly deplorable as life in *Animal House* might have been, real brotherhoods were formed. That, of course, is the positive of Greek life.

I have many friends that, to this day, I would unabashedly call brothers. People from all walks of life. For a kid from Iowa, with brothers from the Southside of Chicago or Spanish Harlem, or Jersey, or Vegas, I began to see an inkling of my true place in this world.

Yet, despite evidence of a much broader horizon, I maintained a big fish persona. I managed to retain this supreme sense of confidence for many years. It's true what they say: "Ignorance is bliss."

There are many tales of utter depravity during my college days. I often told my Navy compadres that undergrad was the place where I grew up. Had I been in the service as an enlisted sailor, I probably would've ended up in Ft. Leavenworth.

After a disastrous sophomore year, despite some internal resistance and continued rebellion, I grew up. When I finished that terrible year, I did manage to complete all my extra credit for macro, and I did ace the final. From a points perspective, I'm pretty sure I made an A. On my report card, I received a B. Lesson learned. It was the only B in my major. If I had not cheated, if I'd just done the work—not phoned it in—I would have had a 4.0 in my major.

Chapter Four: Childish Things

In typical Goldilocks fashion, if my freshman year encompassed too much seriousness and my sophomore year too much revelry, my junior year was just right. I had attained a level of maturity befitting an upper-level student. Though my dreams of pitching at Yankee Stadium still lived, the realization that a plan B might be necessary had started to invade my psyche.

The names of my heroes gradually changed, and I didn't know or fully understand why. Names like Catfish and Thurman morphed to those of Winston and Theodore and, later, Chuck and Pappy.

I'd finished my deep dive into anything associated with Camelot. Instead of assuming the inspirational aspects of our nation's thirty-fifth president, I was enamored by all the things that made JFK, JFK. I saw dashing images of a young Naval Officer in his liberty whites, a preppy undergrad at the tiller of a small boat. I saw a vigorous youth playing football out on the lawn or the politician puffing on a Cuban. I saw a man of letters and a man of adventure. I saw the great good, as well as the flawed humanity. I tried to gravitate toward them, but alas, I believe only the flawed humanity part gained purchase.

The philosophy of his doctrine was not disagreeable either. Although, from an economic standpoint, I'd become a fiscal conservative. The Kennedy tax cut of nineteen sixty-four—passed well after his assassination—was, in my mind, a stroke of genius.

In the fall of that year, nineteen eighty-four, I voted for Ronald Reagan. Like many of his era, he had professed loyalty to FDR. Now he'd become the voice of conservatism, stating, "He hadn't changed; the Democratic Party had."

On the career front, I figured it was time to start thinking about what I would do for a living. I began by figuring my most likely avenues for economic viability and happiness—sadly, in that order—would be something in Finance or Banking. There were serious problems with this plan—flaws in my logic that would reveal themselves nearly two decades hence.

In those days, the economy was a shamble. Stagflation was what they called it. Fed Chair, Paul Volker, had broken inflation's back by providing us a dose of the most terrible medicine. With interest rates at astronomical levels, Volker's plan worked. It was painful, though. As such, prospects for a job were scarce.

One concern was open for business. President Reagan was rebuilding America's armed forces, and jobs were plentiful there. Just like that, in the fall of my junior year, my long-dormant penchant for all things military—specifically military aviation—was re-stoked. The embers of a dream began anew.

I started investigating the various options concerning a career in the military. I had this wacky idea that I wanted to fly fighters. That eliminated the Army. While they do possess many aircraft, most are rotary-winged. My first choice was the Marine Corps. Why? The reasons should have been many. A rich history. The fact that they did have fighters. Semper Fi. No. I thought they had cool uniforms. They do, by the way. It's not a good reason on which to fashion one's life. I wasn't totally sold on the concept. It was a solid plan B, though. I was going to give it serious consideration and began by calling the local USMC recruiter. Of course, my focus, despite all the distractions, was still baseball. I had not quite relinquished that dream. Yet, at five feet ten inches and a hundred seventy pounds dripping wet, I was banking heavily on a late growth spurt to bolster a less than stellar fastball.

Though I'd dipped my toe in the water, I hadn't fully committed to the USMC. See, I had a hernia. More importantly, I knew that until it was repaired, no branch of the military would touch me. I met the local recruiter and was given a brief rundown of the happenings at Quantico. It sounded awesome. I shook the Staff Sergeant's hand and promised that I would contact him after my surgery.

I stopped reading. I'd been a voracious reader as a freshman and sophomore, but fighter pilots are required to have 20/20 vision. I only read when it was required.

Of course, with a double major, more than plenty was required.

Next, I met with the Navy recruiter. I heard words I'd never heard before, words like gouge, geedunk, and chit. There was a poster of a Tomcat, nose on, on the office wall. The Navy claimed it had more tactical fixed-wing aircraft than the Air Force. That first meeting sold me. I didn't sign anything, but the Officer Recruiter, a Surface Warfare Officer, promised he would get me a ride in a trainer.

A few days later, I called the US Air Force Recruiter. My goal was to set up an appointment to discuss a future in the Air Force. The guy asked about my grade point average, then my major. I told him.

"We're looking for people to fly our airplanes that have had a more math-centric education. You know, engineers and the like; a Bachelor of Science, and not of Arts."

Slowly, over the course of that fall, a plan began to coalesce. The Air Force recruiter was a jerk. I never contacted him again. I suddenly warmed to the idea of landing on ships. Anyone could land on a runway. Marines wore the same wings as the Navy. They were required to demonstrate the ability to land on aircraft carriers, and they had the coolest uniforms.

I made the appointment to have my hernia surgery over Christmas break. Yet, during this time, the Navy guy kept calling me. He was friendly. He seemed quite sincere. Knowing what I know now, his seemingly genuine concern for me was simply because I would eventually help him meet a quota.

Yet another issue loomed. Things were not as clear as they seemed. There was a girl. I was in the fall semester of my junior year, but I'd fallen, and now the decision to pursue either path, that of flying in the military or playing baseball, seemed selfish. That said, I was on a mission. In the narcissistic fog of my youth, my life's goal was neatly encompassed in either pursuit. Thankfully, the lady that in a little more than a year would be my wife was game. I think of other girls that I might have pursued. Looking back, I don't believe marriage to any of them would have lasted.

Chapter Five:

There's Gonna Be a Fight!

In 1983, I attained a level of maturity. I was a twenty-one-year-old man, but despite attaining a modicum of good sense, I still had a wagonload of oats to sew.

On a nondescript evening in early December, I'd just finished my homework. One of my fraternity brothers yelled from across the hall, "Hey Kendall, Letterman's about to start. Come check it out." In those days, I'd relegated drunken revelry until after "The David Letterman Show" on account of my newfound sense of responsibility. That evening, I had decided I would stay in. I'd already donned my jammies, which consisted of surgical pants and a t-shirt. I was just settling down with two of my fraternity brothers for what was fast becoming an evening ritual, watching this relatively new show called "David Letterman," when one of our brothers came running in yelling, "THERE'S GONNA BE A FIGHT!"

"Where?" someone asked.

"YARD!" he screamed over his shoulder as he continued his mission. You would have thought he was warning of British Invasion.

Like all able-bodied minutemen, we sprang into action. Everyone flew to their dressers. Nobody wanted to miss a second of the fight. Like a pack of bloodthirsty Romans bound for the Colosseum, we were giddy with anticipation. I recall being momentarily airborne as I pulled on my jeans.

As is my fashion, I was the last person out the door. I soon realized that I hadn't missed the fight. I was going to be in it.

It seems that three or four football players were holding their weekly radio show on the campus radio station. It was a sports-centric program with a call-in portion built in. The show was being held on a single phone line. Earlier that evening, one of my fraternity brothers, a communications major, who hosted a popular music hour, had called in to remind the football players to announce his program during one of their commercial breaks. The guy was notoriously late with his phone bill, and his service had recently been cut off. The call that evening had come from my room.

"Hey, man, can I use your phone?" he'd asked.

"Local?"

"Just calling the radio station to ask them to announce my show tomorrow."

"No problem," I said.

The call was made. I continued my studies.

The campus phone system, in those days separate from the community, was antiquated at best. For those not of a certain age, this was the pre-cell phone era. If both parties didn't properly disconnect, the line remained open. I had this funky phone that hung on the wall and rested in a holster-like apparatus. If not properly seated, the phone didn't hang up. When my fraternity brother used my phone to announce his show, he failed to disconnect, thus ruining the last hour of the sports call-in show. While I studied quietly in my room, four football players sat across campus seething. They took turns listening to relative silence in search of any clue to find the son-of-a-bitch who'd ruined their show. At roughly ten-thirty, they heard someone say faintly, "Hey Kendall, Letterman's about to start. Come check it out." From that moment, my fate was sealed. My face was going to have a violent rendezvous with destiny, or at least the knuckles of an irate backup tight end.

I stepped outside to assume my position at the crowd's periphery. I wanted an optimal vantage point from which to view the impending action. Much to my surprise, individuals forming the perimeter gave way. Suddenly, my plan to be a spectator shifted as I looked at the ring surrounding me and listened to a big man screaming obscenities.

For the life of me, I could not fathom why this man was so mad, and more importantly, mad at me.

I don't remember exactly what the man said. I remember only that it was venomous and filthy. He got right in my face. He was a head taller than me, and I could smell liquor on his breath. I do not remember being scared. I remember thinking how utterly absurd this whole situation was. I could not fathom why this was happening.

Though this person was much larger, I wasn't afraid. My father had taught me the rudiments of boxing, and I'd never been bested in a fight. Oh, did I mention my last fight was in seventh grade? I'm not a fighter, yet I was about to trade punches with someone far beyond my weight class.

This situation was so strange. I didn't understand why this guy was screaming obscenities in my face. He was literally spitting mad. I understood the futility of trying to reason with this drunk, and when he started in on my mother, I'd had enough.

I hadn't had a fight in a good long while, but apparently, the moment you lay hands on your opponent, the fight's on. Who knew? I was sick of this Neanderthal's tripe and shoved him lightly as I started to turn away.

The next thing I recall was watching a ropey sinew of my blood fly out into the snow-covered yard. I stumbled back but managed to stay upright, and I remember wondering why the snow all around me was pink. A terrible battle ensued. I'd like to tell you I gave as good as I got. That would be a bald-faced lie. Still, considering that I was fighting well above my weight class, I will say that I acquitted myself reasonably well.

I suffered from a badly cut lip, the result of the permanent retainer I had in those days. That was the cause of all the bloodshed, the clear majority anyway. Some blood spilled was the result of a bite on my bicep. The fight ended suddenly when my opponent threw a big roundhouse, which I ducked. The punch landed with a sickening thud against the brick wall I was holding up.

I think this resulted in a broken bone in his hand. I considered it a win. Other football players were circling like sharks, ready to clean up what was left of me. Yet several of my fraternity brothers were football players too. The fight ended with two lines of exceptionally large people facing one another. Two of my brothers ushered me to the emergency room to get my lip stitched up and a tetanus shot for the bite.

Days later, after he'd pieced the story together, the guy that I fought—okay, the guy that beat me up—apologized for his idiocy. I said, "Don't worry about it." Honestly, it took me half a decade to forgive him in my heart.

The opportunity to test one's mettle in pitched combat, sanctioned or not, was, in my mind, a way to measure a man's worth. I now believe the fight that night may have been a message. A message that I was too immature to interpret. In battle, there is no glory, and there are no winners.

The opportunity to test one's mettle in match combat, sanctioned or not, was in my mind, a way to measure a man's worth. I now believe the fight that night may have been a message. A message that I was too immature to interpret. In battle, there is no glory, and there are no winners.

Chapter Six:

Conventional Wisdom

A week later, I was on Christmas break. I had surgery during my first week at home. I'd just gotten stitches removed from my mouth and now had staples a bit lower. Unable to work out, and since it was the height of eating season, I quickly gained ten or fifteen pounds. It's the heaviest I've ever been.

I'd lettered my freshman year. But the school had hired a new coach, and under new management, I mostly rode the pine my sophomore year. Sadly, I did the same in my junior year. It was still a few months until I realized that I would never be a professional athlete. I guess I'm not that smart. Yet, the seed of a feeling had begun to germinate within.

We began baseball practice in earnest immediately upon our return from Christmas break. Sadly, there's not a lot for me to report on the baseball front. At best, I could be defined as a middle-reliever and/or utility player. I played in the outfield for a few innings. I played first base, maybe twice. I pitched countless innings in the bullpen. Yet I only actually pitched in a handful of games.

True to his word, the Navy Recruiter arranged a ride in a T-34 Mentor. This was an avgas-powered prop plane. The training version that I would later fly, the T-34C Turbo-Mentor, was a turboprop, and as such, it flew more like a jet. Yet, on that cold sunny afternoon, from a little grass strip, we launched. It felt like I'd won the lottery. Before we touched down, I knew what I was meant to do.

My recruiter was a great salesman. He didn't bug me continuously, but he didn't let me wither on the vine either. He would check in and occasionally offer pertinent facts. I had not yet called the USMC recruiter back. I planned to—I really did—but the Navy guy kept sending me posters, bumper stickers, and other such geedunk.[1] The final nail in the coffin was when he sent me this little "by the numbers" marketing slick. It essentially broke down how many tactical jets each branch of the military flew. It also showed how many helicopters the Marines had. I am not a smart guy, but it was clear that if I wanted to fly fighters, the Marine Corps was not the best option, cool uniforms or not.

[1] Geedunk is a Navy term originally derived from the British Royal Navy in India. It connotes cheap novelty paraphernalia that is often used as a promotional tool for advertising some cause or concern. It is generally some cheap gift you receive – perhaps to commemorate an event. Alternatively, a geedunk bar (/ˈgiːdʌŋk/ GHEE-dunk) is the canteen or snack bar of a large vessel of the United States Navy or the United States Coast Guard; thus, geedunk are the items sold within (candy).

As an underclassman, one of my chief diversions had been that of reading. My penchant for Economics, Business, Finance, and, more specifically, Equities found me devouring books on the subject, charting mock portfolios, and generally finding out as much as I could about how to trade stocks. In 1982, my parents bought me "The Intelligent Investor," and soon after, "Securities Analysis" by Benjamin Graham. Graham had been Warren Buffet's favorite professor at Princeton. At that time, the lure of easy money piqued my curiosity. The notion that you could make money by simply investing was almost inconceivable. Truth told, though, I had neither the drive nor the intellect for it. I told myself that one day, after time in the military, I would always be able to settle down as a respectable stockbroker.

As a young man, however, I did not want to sit behind a desk. I wanted a job that required me to wear a helmet to work. In my mind, that would either be a baseball helmet or a crash helmet.

The spring became summer, and I soon found myself starting my final summer at Mickey Owen Baseball School. At age twenty-one, I was no longer a counselor responsible for good order in my cabin, as well as field maintenance. I was a coach. I was earning over two hundred bucks a week, plus room and board. Moreover, I wasn't just a coach. I got to play several games a week. By July, I was playing the best baseball of my life. Over many summers, I had learned more about the game and about pitching than most people will ever know. I ran every day. I may have been in the best shape of my life. Since my job included room and board, I was saving like mad. I was saving to buy a diamond.

After my boss's speech suggesting that I shift my focus from player to coach, conventional wisdom suggested that I take some entry-level finance job—at a bank perhaps—or the Assistant Coaching job at the Junior College level. After all, I was only a year from being a husband. Yet, in a move that would have made Admiral Farragut[2] proud, I decided to damn conventional wisdom, full speed ahead. I was going to be a Naval Aviator.

By the end of the summer, I'd saved enough to purchase a decent-sized diamond. I could nearly sprint around the little road that ringed the camp. I'd made peace with the notion that I would never step across the foul line at Yankee Stadium. Not as a player, anyway. As summer waned, I showed the movie an "Officer and a Gentleman" on VHS to my boss and mentor, foolishly thinking Hollywood could accurately depict the next phase of my life.

On my last day in the Ozarks, I went around the camp, reminiscing about the summers I'd spent there. I looked at the fields of green and thought about the languorous contentment of a tangerine sun on a saffron horizon, the dog days of summer when the ping of aluminum was the dominant noise. I also thought about the friends I'd known. I said goodbye to my boss, my friend, and my mentor. As I write this, I realize I owe

[2] Union Admiral David Farragut gave the general order to his ships at the Battle of Mobile Bay (1864), "Damn the torpedoes, full speed ahead."

him a phone call. We've stayed in touch for over thirty years. Someday, I hope to visit him. We haven't seen one another since that day.

In the fall of nineteen eighty-four, I began my senior year at William Penn. I'd been a novice model builder—at least intermittently—since I was a little kid. Iowa winters are an excellent time to build models. My genre was always airplanes, with a heavy emphasis on military aircraft, specifically fighters. That year, when I had finished decorating my room, models of fighters hung from my ceiling. Admittedly, when I'd finished, the room looked more like the abode of a prepubescent child than that of a college senior. I didn't care. With my proclivity to decorate with models of fast movers, I'd boldly declared my intentions.

On September 3rd, 1984, I asked Sherri to marry me. Sometimes, thinking of her life, I wonder if it might have been better—for her—if she'd turned and ran. For me, though, thank God she said yes.

I cautioned my new fiancée that I was seriously considering a military career and that I wanted to be a Naval Aviator. I was saying that our future depended not on our collective willingness to compromise but on her willingness to be a part of my manifest destiny.

him a phone call. We've stayed in touch for over thirty years. Someday, I hope to visit him. We haven't seen one another since that day.

In the fall of nineteen eighty-four, I began my senior year at William Penn. I'd been a novice model builder—at least intermittently—since I was a little kid. Iowa winters are an excellent time to build models. My genre was always airplanes, with a heavy emphasis on military aircraft, specifically fighters. That year, [illegible] had finished decorating my room: models of fighters hung from my ceiling. Admittedly, when I'd finished, the room looked more like the abode of a prepubescent child than that of a college senior. I didn't care. With my proclivity to decorate with models of "fast movers," I'd boldly declared my intentions.

On September 8th, 1984, I asked Sherri to marry me. Sometimes, thinking of her life, I wonder if it might have been better for her—if she'd turned and run. For me, though, thank God she said yes.

I cautioned my new fiancée that I was seriously considering a military career, and that I wanted to be a Naval Aviator. I was saying that our future depended not on our collective willingness to compromise but on her willingness to be a part of my singular destiny.

Chapter Seven: Planning

Plans for a June wedding began. Sherri made the arrangements for a wedding in our hometown. Yes, we had dated in high school, rekindled our romance in college, and were now planning to make it permanent. Thankfully, much of the pre-arranging minutiae was left to my future wife as I, a slightly younger man, was still thoroughly ensconced in the throes of my senior year of college.

Meanwhile, plans were progressing for a future in Naval Aviation. While my betrothed explored the beauty and majesty of a religion that I'd taken for granted all my life, I was plotting a grandiose strategy for world domination. My career in Naval Aviation was simply the launch pad. I'd like to say that these words are merely literary hyperbole. Unfortunately, that would not be accurate. At age twenty-two, I'd already planned my future. I would build my own Camelot.

In November of 1984, I signed a deferred entry contract to the Navy's aviation program. I would attend Aviation Officer Candidate School sometime after graduation. The beauty of delayed entry was that my years of service would start immediately, yet I wasn't committed to serving. While I had signed, I had not raised my right hand. In keeping with the general theme for a prospective aviator, quitting is painless. Failure is painless. If you're not fully committed, and if you don't truly want it, the Navy doesn't want you driving their airplanes. There are several jumping-off points.

My recruiter told me that the way things were shaping up, it looked as though I would not be called upon to begin AOCS (Aviation Officer's Candidate School) until sometime in the fall of 1985. He said that it could perhaps be sooner if I chose to be a Naval Flight Officer (NFO).

That meant that a honeymoon was conceivable. I began planning a trip to Cozumel.

Meanwhile, I had become an elder statesman of sorts within my fraternity, having served in nearly every position of authority, including two terms as the organization's President. Additionally, I was elected as President of our school's Inter-Fraternity Council (IFC). This position would eventually present me with a tremendous moral dilemma and lead to an interesting conflict of interest.

My need to lead, to be noticed, and to be at the epicenter of the happenings within my growing sphere of influence has led me to try and accomplish many things during my college career. That eventually led to me being named to *Who's Who Among Students in American Universities & Colleges*. Truth told, a fraternity brother—the eventual best man at my wedding—spearheaded the effort to submit our names for consideration. Today Carlos is a high-powered executive. He has a great family and, by all earthly measures, is a mover and shaker.

The focus of my early life was beginning to coalesce into something resembling success. The upward mobility that I craved would be possible, but first, I still needed to be a hero in combat. I began to worry that there would never be another significant war. Of course, if life played out per my plan, perhaps another war was unnecessary. No one would dare question the gallantry of a Naval Aviator. Despite the current drought in world conflict, I believed that a stint living aboard (and landing on) an Aircraft Carrier would cement my standing as a legitimate hero.

In the springtime, I played every day. No more riding the pine. My baseball career, which began with some promise at age seven in left field, would end there as well with little fanfare.

Back home, wedding plans continued. Sherri, my fiancée, completed her catechesis. She had grown up in the Methodist tradition. Things were shaping up nicely for a June wedding.

In early spring, I was in the final throes of a life that had been built around organized athletics. Early in the season, the team's head coach had called a meeting to elect team captains. Much to my surprise and his, the team nearly unanimously elected two long-time benchwarmers as co-captains for the spring season. It may have been the result of simple pity, or perhaps my other teammates were paying homage to the virtue of patience and perseverance—read foolhardy determination—but in the end, much to our coach's chagrin, Ozzy and I were named team co-captains.

We had a stretch of reasonably warm weather. On a weekend in March, we—that is, my fraternity—decided that a party was in order. We were having difficulty finding a venue. In an alcohol-fueled flash of brilliance, someone suggested that—what with the spate of warm weather—we should consider a daytime party at a local park shelter. A vote was taken, the motion carried, and the inertia of our plan quickly gained momentum. Flyers went out, kegs were ordered, and garbage cans of hooch were mixed. The campus was abuzz with the radical notion of a daytime party. Did I mention that our parties were legendary? The concept of an afternoon at the park was opening a whole new genre of debauchery.

As President, I oversaw procuring the venue. In those days—for good reason—all the organizations in town were reluctant to rent facilities to us. The park, after hard negotiations, only agreed to rent us the outdoor portion of one of their indoor/outdoor shelters. The price was right. The weather had been downright balmy for several days. We wrote them a check. I shook a man's hand and agreed to the terms.

I went to school in Iowa, pre-global warming. One could make a strong argument that it was quite possibly the worst weather on planet earth. It might be colder in

Des Moines than Siberia in January and hotter than Djibouti a scant six months later. As you may have guessed by now, it was cool that afternoon. Of course, alcohol would keep us warm, or so we thought.

Brothers and patrons all drank as much as we could as fast as we could. Yet we were getting cold. By two-thirty, it was apparent that our party was on life support. Some people had already left. Other folks were contemplating an exit. Something had to be done.

Operating under the "better to ask forgiveness than permission" dictum, I made a call that we should open the indoor portion of the shelter—the portion that we were specifically prohibited from using. In an alcohol-induced stupor, I tested the door. It was locked, but the door jam was a rather flimsy contraption. With minimal effort, I managed to force the door. The party instantly turned from a sad little gathering, dwindling with the sun, to another memorable event for which our parties were famous.

I was a hero, a man of action, and a leader of mythical proportions. I was greeted by everybody as I walked across the campus. I loved academia. I loved my time at William Penn. It's interesting that even now, I'm able to romanticize the occasion. The event wasn't over, though, as I would soon find out.

At the next Inter-Fraternity Council meeting, the campus disciplinary board presented an airtight case against a fraternity that had been accused of breaking into a shelter to hold a party. As the organization's leader, in what can only be described as divine irony, I presided over the punishment phase of my own fraternity. Talk about a "fox guarding the henhouse" moment. I, the person responsible for the break-in, would now be responsible for assigning punishment to the perpetrators (me). Yet, I would be foiled by *Robert's Rules of Order*. I attempted to assuage the room's pervading sentiment, but as luck would have it, the President can only suggest motions. That said, the act could have meant my fraternity's ultimate demise. In the end, I managed to guide my fellow Greeks to a suspension of two years. It was still, quite nearly, the death knell for my fraternity.

I was just forty-eight hours from posting my deposit for our honeymoon down in Cozumel when my recruiter called.

"Hey, great news."

"What's that?" I asked.

"We've got a class date."

"Great! When do I start?" I asked, certain the answer would be sometime in the fall.

"I've got you a start date of June twenty-third," he said.

Silence reigned for several seconds. "I thought you'd said I wouldn't start until the fall?"

"Probably. I said,... *probably*," he added once again.

"But I'm getting married on the eighth. I was planning my honeymoon for the sixteenth."

"You haven't put down a deposit yet, have you?"

"Not yet, but..."

"Well, great. I don't see a problem. Look, I know it's earlier than we planned, but these things are sort of beyond our control. We're starting a class every week. SECNAV is trying to adhere to President Reagan's plan for a six-hundred ship Navy. You know what that means, right?"

"What?" I asked in a tedious monotone, already thinking of ways to explain our canceled honeymoon.

"If the Navy is twice as big, we need more carriers. More carriers mean more airplanes. Going early seems unfortunate, but actually, the timing is perfect."

Perfect, I thought.

Chapter Eight
Transitions

On May 7th, 1985, I graduated from William Penn College. I had played in the last officially sanctioned sporting event of my life days earlier. On June 8th, Sherri and I were married. On June sixteenth, pulling a U-Haul behind our Monte Carlo, we left for Pensacola, Florida.

Two days later, sheets of rain pelted our windshield as we rolled down Barrancas Avenue toward Naval Air Station Pensacola. Naval bases are not typically surrounded by posh real estate. As we tooled past biker bars and tattoo parlors, I glanced over at my new bride. Tears were streaming down her cheeks as she looked at her new life. Even with my stunning lack of empathy, I recognized that this day represented a drastic change for a young woman who'd only been out of Iowa a handful of times in her life.

The rain had let up a bit as we parked in front of a building marked "Induction." My new bride's waterworks had also diminished significantly.

I said, "We'll just check in to see if the real estate liaison has some suggestions for rental apartments." We held hands as we crossed the street. It was a Sunday morning.

Sunday was the day that new candidates checked in. I knew this, but of course, my own check-in date was not until next week. We wanted to get Sherri set up with a place before I began training. We walked into the little building, still holding hands. It had a narrow green hallway and receiving desk off to the right. It looked more like the entrance to a police precinct. There was a large individual in a white uniform behind that desk. He was barking commands at a recruit who stood before him. I let Sherri's hand go and approached the desk.

I'd taken two steps when he looked at me with venomous contempt and shouted, "UP AGAINST THE BULKHEAD, SLIME!" I hurriedly complied. I glanced back at Sherri just in time to see her exit the building.

I watched the man inducting people and started to get mad. This guy was a nobody. He was a senior candidate. Exactly like I'd be in a scant few weeks. He had three bars on his collar. Apparently, he hadn't gotten the memo that I would be swinging by to visit the real estate liaison. I vowed that I would not allow myself to be molded into an unthinking automaton like the kid behind the counter.

When it became my turn, the guy said, "STEP FORWARD, SLIME."

I didn't consider myself slimy, but as I would soon discover, I was a slimy civilian, the lowest form of scum typically found on the dark side of bottom dwellers.

I stepped up to the counter.

"NAME."

"I'm not a check-in," I blurted.

The man looked at me. He seemed perplexed. He was big, but he looked like a kid just out of college, which he was.

"I'll be checking in next week. I'm just here to meet with the real estate liaison. I want to get my wife set up in an apartment before I start."

He was now nearly apoplectic in his current state of confusion. After an uncomfortable period of being stared at, the man responsible for induction picked up the phone.

After a short conversation and still holding the receiver, he said, "The liaison will see you in ten minutes. Both of you," he added, sounding almost human.

I found my bride pacing nervously up and down the sidewalk across the street. It was a gray day, and rain still dripped from the pines as I stepped onto the curb and watched Sherri approach. It was obvious that she had been crying again.

"What'd they say? They're not going to keep you now, are they?" she asked.

"No, honey, they're not keeping me today," I said. "They thought I was a new check-in for the class that'll start tomorrow. I explained it to the guy behind the desk. We meet with the real estate liaison in a few minutes."

"They're very polite here," she said.

"How's that?"

"Well, that guy," she said, pointing to a man in khakis walking away from us, "just said, 'good morning, ma'am.'"

At this stage, neither of us recognized a standard military greeting.

So, rather inauspiciously, we began our military career. Of course, in those days, I'm sure I would have said my career, but Sherri, not I, would run our household, raise our children, and make our home. In other words, while I was out there having the time of my life, she would be relegated to the hard work of running a household.

We did meet the liaison that morning, and we did find an apartment on the north side of Pensacola. Presumably, I would end up at Naval Air Station Whiting Field, near Milton, Florida, for primary flight school, which was several miles to the north. As such, living on the north side of town would prevent us from having to move after Aviation Officer Candidate School.

That gave us the entire week to explore our new surroundings. We decided to check out the beach. The gulf coast has some of the prettiest beaches on the planet. Sugar white sand stretched endlessly toward the horizon. Paradise. Sort of.

We put our blanket out and staked our claim, so to speak. Sherri began unpacking various beach accouterments, and I immediately turned toward the water's edge.

"Where you going?" she said.

"I'm going swimming," I said.

It was hot, and I wondered as I picked my way through the dead jellyfish littering the beach why more of the idiots baking in the sun didn't partake in a refreshing dip. I dove in and began swimming out to sea. I'd gone about sixty feet when something terribly painful—I mean, take your breath away kind of painful—slid across the right side of my face, down my neck, and along my torso. It stung worse than any wasp or bee that I'd ever known. It burned and felt electric at the same time. I turned back toward the shore.

I plainly detected the disdain of local beachgoers as I reached the water's edge. I'm pretty sure I saw a couple of them shaking their heads. Some of the locals felt sorry for me, having spied the damage that the jellyfish had done. People were suggesting home remedies, and one lady brought over a bottle of meat tenderizer, suggesting we sprinkle it on liberally. I did so, thinking, who's the idiot now?

Class Three Zero Eight Five began on June twenty-third, in the year of Our Lord, Nineteen, Eighty-Five. On the day that I met our DI (Drill Instructor), I briefly considered the wisdom of my chosen path. Our DI was a Gunnery Sergeant in the United States Marine Corps. All the DIs were Gunnery Sergeants, save one. He was a Staff Sergeant. It might be a good time to note that there are three Departments in the D.O.D. They are Army, Air Force, and Navy. The Marine Corps is in the

Department of the Navy. I was not an academy grad, but I believe students must declare, in their junior year, whether they will be Naval Officers or Marine Corps Officers. At any rate, if you're still confused, check out the movie *An Officer and a Gentleman*, starring Richard Gere, Debra Winger, and Louis Gossett Jr. as the DI, a Marine Corps Gunny.

That next morning at 0430, a garbage can was hurled down the passageway. With that clanging din, the mania began. We sprang from our racks and fell into formation. There were several blue-legged Marines stalking about. None of them was my drill instructor. He was far down the line yelling in a booming voice at our slovenly appearance. He sounded as though he were nine feet tall. I knew better than to look. My eyes remained locked in front.

It was probably day three before I finally mustered the nerve for a fleeting glance. Our Drill Instructor, the man I thought had to be at least six and a half feet tall, was about five feet six, maybe.

That morning started with PT (physical training), then we spent some time learning how to march. Then seventy-three of us marched over to the Naval Aerospace Medical Institute (NAMI), where we were put through a battery of very thorough exams. Some candidates who had marched over as would-be pilots marched back as Naval Flight Officers. Other candidates did not want to be back-seaters and left the program, and still, others were eliminated. There were fifty-three of us as we marched to the barbershop. Several of us would-be aviators had gotten the old NAMI whammy.

Minutes later, once-flowing locks lay in piles on the barbershop floor. Fifty-three "cue balls" stood quietly under a now scorching sun. It had been a whirlwind of a day, and we had yet to have lunch. Our Drill Instructor apparently took mercy on us, saying, "PAH-RADE REST FALL OUT! Y'ALL GOT FIVE MIKES TO MILL ABOUT SMARTLY."

We broke ranks to make the acquaintance of one another. One of the guys behind me was crying sloppily. Others were doing their best to console him.

"This place sucks," he blubbered. "I'm gonna DOR (drop on request). Maybe the bank will hire me back."

This was too much. I could no longer stand idly by and said, "Gee, ya think? You look like a fucking convict. If you were gonna quit, why didn't you do it before they shaved your head?"

That garnered a few chuckles, but the man at whose expense I'd made this little joke had become inconsolable. He was gone by lunchtime. I never knew his name.

For the next thirteen weeks, we would learn the intricacies of becoming Naval Officers, and not only that but prospective Aviators. We drilled for hours on end. I began to wonder if we would end up guarding the Tomb of the Unknowns. We spent considerable time doing push-ups and other forms of physical training (PT).

While I learned about meteorology, aerodynamics, and navigation, my new bride began searching for work and making our house a home. Of course, she was doing this all by herself.

I, on the other hand, became intimately familiar with the O-course (obstacle) and the C-course (cross-country), the pull-up bar, and the thing I dreaded most; the pool.

Growing up, while others vacationed at various lakes, I had spent nearly every waking moment of every summer since age seven playing baseball. Consequently, I could not swim very well.

Naval officer candidates who can't swim aren't unheard of, but if they also happen to be prospective aviators, they're not in the business very long. This would become my first major hurdle. I did not enter the Navy totally unprepared. I had taken a swim class in college. I thought I was ready.

To continue in the program, candidates had to swim a mile in full flight gear, demonstrate proficiency in the four survival strokes (crawl, breast, side, and backstroke), jump from a thirty-foot platform and swim across the pool underwater, tread water for five minutes, and drown-proof for another five.

After a week, those struggling in the pool were identified, and a remedial swim class was offered. I was in that class. We were referred to as "swim rocks." In those days, I was solid. The label was indeed apropos. Consequently, my natural resting state was a hovering position several feet below the surface. I soon gave the remedial swim class a new moniker. I called it drowning practice.

In that time and place, dedication, devotion to duty, and, dare I say, personal valor were on full display in a swimming pool at the birthplace of Naval Aviation. No one had fired a shot in anger. No one had wrestled a disabled bird onto a pitching deck on an ink-black night. No, we just fought tooth and tongue against the inevitable exhaustion of treading water in flight gear. It isn't that hard if you know how, but at least twice weekly, instructors would fish some poor bastard out of the pool. On one occasion, a lifeless student was noticed lingering near the bottom. He was pulled onto the pool deck by rescue divers who were there to protect aviation candidates. Side note: We were so focused on someday earning "wings of gold" that we'd all learn to tread water or die trying. Divers were there mainly to protect Aviation Officer Candidates from themselves.

The seemingly dead man was all blue after an extended interval of oxygen deprivation. After a few seconds of not breathing, the kid—lying on his side—spilled water from his lungs. After another moment, he sputtered and then coughed. They hauled him off in an ambulance. We never saw him again.

Domino's Pizza delivers anywhere. Apparently, some numbskull questioned this axiom and ordered a large pepperoni delivered to his room on the third floor of Batt Two (the building housing members of the second battalion). Sadly, that mouth breather was in my class. That lunacy ended up costing us. There was at least a slim chance of weekend liberty at week four. It didn't happen. No matter, classes seldom got liberty that early. Our next opportunity was week six. Unfortunately, our Drill Instructor happened to be inspecting our passageway when—in week five—he spied the pizza delivery guy knocking discreetly on a door down the hall. After that little escapade, my new bride and I would only see one another for two hours on Sunday afternoons. We were relegated to several weeks of clandestine PDA (Public Displays of Affection) along the sea wall.

That wasn't the end of it, though. Early that next week was a "black flag day." That's when the combination of ambient temperature and humidity is dangerously high. The condition is denoted by a black flag. Our DI, a sadistic out-of-the-box thinker, had us doing pushups in the tiny, air-conditioned entry foyer of the battalion. There were still over forty of us in that little space. So, we did a few pushups. Big deal, right?

When the afternoon had ended, our DI made his exit, and those of us still capable of walking got up and began sweeping the floor clear of salt. I recall thinking that it looked as though there'd been a light dusting of snow. It wasn't snow, though. Rather it was the remnants of our sweat, now dried, that had poured from our bodies that afternoon. We'd done over two thousand pushups that day. Expensive pizza.

Despite this bump in the road, our DI was beginning to meld us into finely-honed would-be Naval Officers. We could bounce loose change off our beds, we could polish brass to a mirrored finish, and our boots were spit-shined. And despite hours in the classroom learning about occluded fronts or L/D Max (ell over dee max), our bodies had begun to change. Funny what a few thousand pushups, sit-ups, pullups, miles, and laps in a pool will do. In those days, I had a thirty-one-inch waist and a forty-two-inch chest.

Still, I had drowning practice every day. I called it that because, on more than one occasion, my body, at the point of exhaustion, physically gave up. I watched the surface recede as I sunk toward the bottom. I wondered how my widowed bride would fare. I decided that drowning, once accepted, wasn't such a terrible way to go. Inevitably, right before I was about to succumb to my fate and suck in a big old lung full of agua, a grappling hook would latch hold of my SV-2 (survival vest) and pull me to the surface. Once again, I'd stop thinking about my spouse and think only about my failure.

Challenges like that are commonplace when it comes to achieving some great goal. We strive and reach, and goals seemingly impossible become possible. Things that appear beyond our reach are attained if we want them. Seemingly insurmountable barriers were only tiny speed bumps on the way to our destiny. It may seem corny, but Winston Churchill had it right when he said, "Never, never, never quit."

After several weeks of struggling and frequent brushes with my own demise, I discovered something utterly amazing: treading water while vertical was much more difficult than if you oriented your body horizontally. This obvious point allowed me to pass out of "swim rock" class that same week. More challenges lay ahead, though.

thinking about my doubts and think only about my future.

Challenges like these are commonplace when it comes to achieving some great goal. We strive and reach, and goals seemingly impossible become possible. Things that appear beyond our reach are attained if we want them. Seemingly insurmountable barriers were yesterday's speed bumps on the way to our destiny. It may seem corny, but Winston Churchill had it right when he said, "Never, never, never quit."

After several weeks of struggling and frequent brushes with my own demise, I discovered something utterly amazing: treading water while vertical was much more difficult than if you oriented your body horizontally. This obvious point allowed me to pass out of "swim rock" class that same week. More challenges lay ahead, though.

Chapter Nine:
Flight School

My first weekend liberty happened in week eight. It was during a category one hurricane—our first—that struck Pensacola almost directly. I'm certain the storm caused major damage. It's not my intent to minimize its impact, but it was a cat one, and we lived in a second-floor apartment, and, most importantly, it bought me an extra twenty-four hours of freedom.

My triumph in the pool was short-lived because, in week nine, I injured my knee on the "O" course. I wrenched it badly when I landed awkwardly on the sand as I came off the eight-foot wall. It was originally caused by a football injury in high school. I still nurse a partially torn anterior cruciate ligament. Now, running was out of the question. Normally that meant "G" Company.

"Golf" Company seemed like an abyss, the land of the misfit toys. It was limbo. It was the place you were sent if you were injured. While the rest of the class marched toward graduation and a commission, candidates in "G" company languished, marking time until they were reinserted into a later class. One of the most haunting events of Aviation Officer Candidate School was hearing the announcement "G Company marchin' into chow." It had to be avoided at all costs. The decision was not reached lightly. Input from doctors at NAMI (Naval Aerospace Medical Institute), as well as a panel of Marine Drill Instructors, produced what was essentially the disabled list for AOCS.

When a decision was reached, it was determined that since I'd already qualified on both the "O" and "C" courses, since I'd fully qualified in the pool, and since I could still march and walk, I could continue with my class. This was a huge relief because the prospect of a delay seemed like a failure. This mode of thought would have a far-reaching impact on my life.

The real change, the thing that nearly ended my career before it even started, was such a silly thing. It began with survival training at Eglin Air Force Base. I'm told that it's the place where Army Special Forces do their survival training. Of course, our initial survival is not nearly so intense. I think it was two and one-half days in the wilderness. It was more like an outdoor learning laboratory, a how-to practicum on wilderness survival. I learned many things. I dined on my first rattlesnake; it tasted like chicken.

I enjoyed it, but a couple of weeks later, we were scheduled for the altitude chamber. It's not a big deal, really. You get to experience the effects of hypoxia. It's an insidious sort of thing. We had an hour of training going in. There was a lot of discussion about the way a lack of oxygen would likely manifest itself and how we could recognize it before it killed us. Then the instructor, an aviation physiologist, started talking about the decent portion. During his discussion, he kept warning us, "Look, if you have the sniffles, if you're congested, do not, repeat do not enter the chamber, it's no big deal, you're almost done. We'll just throw you into G Company for a week until you're all clear, and then you can experience the chamber."

All I heard was G COMPANY! I'd be damned if I was going to fall a whole week, maybe more, behind my contemporaries. I was a bit stuffed up. I'd caught a cold while we were on survival training. How bad could it be? I made a monumentally stupid decision. I marched into the chamber.

The ascent was not an issue. Anybody who has flown knows you yawn and swallow a few times, and voilà, the pressure in your sinus cavity and inner ears equalizes.

While at altitude, we did things like play cards, patty cake, etc. The effects of hypoxia were soon plain. Back on oxygen, the hyperbaric chamber was re-pressurized as we simulated our descent. As we descended, I began to feel a slight discomfort in my face. We started to ascend quickly and descend. I momentarily forgot the twinge of pain that I'd felt earlier.

Finally, we began our final descent. At fifteen thousand feet, that little twinge of pain began again. By ten thousand feet, the pain was pronounced. I can gut this out, I thought, grimacing. At eight thousand, the pain was so severe that it felt like someone was stabbing me with an icepick—in my face. I gave the level off signal—as briefed—and aviation physiologists were soon surrounding me. They shot a powerful decongestant up my nose. This process was repeated four times as we tried to get back to ground level. All the while, it felt as if my left maxillary sinus would explode.

Implode is more accurate. Because of the inability to equalize the pressure in my sinus cavity—the result of the cold I'd caught while on survival—the tissue lining my left maxillary sinus violently separated from its inner cavity wall, which is bone. After the chamber, I was rushed to NAMI (Naval Aerospace Medical Institute); suddenly, G Company didn't sound so bad.

I think of my indoctrination into Navy life like the month of March, in like a lion and out... well, you know the rest. Though I felt fine when I handed a silver dollar to my drill instructor after he'd given me my first salute in the military, there was some question as to whether my career would continue.

I spent a couple of weeks mustering with other new officers in limbo. We formed up to listen to someone read the "Plan of the Day," and then we'd all disperse to meet with our doctors for our various ailments. I met with two of them, an orthopedic surgeon and an ENT specialist. I remember the sheer boredom. It was such a waste, but it was only the beginning of a long and arduous journey.

There were no major issues with my knee. I had a partially torn ACL (Anterior Cruciate Ligament) which is what I had been told as a sophomore in high school.

My ENT doctor, on the other hand, was a cum laude graduate of the Josef Mengele[3] School of Medicine.

---

[3] Josef Mengele (German: [ˈmɛŋələ]; 16 March 1911 – 7 February 1979) was a German Schutzstaffel (SS) officer and physician in Auschwitz concentration camp. The real USN Doctor in charge of my care was an ENT Specialist, and shall remain anonymous.

He would spend nearly a year of my life curing me. It took several months before depression gained its grip.

Early on, I was the picture of optimism. After all, my plan was working. I'd taken the first step toward my grandiose scheme. I was a Naval Officer. The notion that a sinus infection might ruin my splendid design was inconceivable.

In fact, after a week of mustering, I launched a brazen campaign to be transferred to NAS Whiting Field. The reasoning was sound. At this juncture, my ailments were considered minor. The first month of primary flight school was ground school. Presumably, by the time I would be allowed near an airplane, my sinus problems would be long gone.

It's amazing what a body gets used to. My torture began with the interesting adaption of a rather innocuous instrument. The doctor suggested a self-fashioned Neti Pot on steroids. The contraption consisted of a standard Water Pik filled with saline and a highly adapted hose on the end. The hose was inserted in one nostril, and all manner of gunk was forcibly expelled out the other. Yeah, it was kind of gross. I did these flushes two or three times a day for two months, maybe more.

The good news is that I had been allowed to start ground school. I no longer had to muster in Pensacola. Now I drove up to NAS Whiting Field every day. I breezed through ground school. I'd like to say that I recognized the impending difficulties that lay ahead. The reality, though, is the glass was still half full. Through my rose-covered goggles, I could only see my eventual success. It was destiny.

I plied my trade as best I could, soaking up every bit of information in a regimented program of self-study. As a relatively successful undergrad, I'd mastered the skill of absorbing large volumes of information.

Once a week, I trekked down to NAMI[4] at NAS Pensacola to get my skull x-rayed. The film showed that the saline rinses were working. Yet, there was a pesky and persistent cloudiness at the bottom of my left maxillary sinus. Dr. Mengele suggested nasal irrigation. I consented.

It was November when I underwent this procedure. I'm not a doctor, so the procedure I describe is subject to the whimsical nature of a lay person's fickle memory. First, the largest needle I've ever seen was inserted—through the back of my left nostril—directly into my left maxillary sinus. This needle was so large that another needle was required to fill the inner void of the main needle so as not to plug it with flesh and bone as it made its way into my noggin. The maxillary sinus is a cavity of bone. Penetration requires a degree of force. I remember the good doctor leaning into the syringe with a two-handed grip and me leaning forward in my chair to counteract the opposing force of the doctor's weight as he wielded his macabre device. There was an audible pop when the needle finally penetrated the bone and entered my maxillary sinus cavity. Next, the inner needle was removed, and saline was flushed directly into my sinus cavity. Then it was sucked out through the syringe along with all manner of nasty green mucus. That said, the doctor's disappointment was evident in that the procedure yielded little extraneous material.

"Based on your x-rays, I would've thought we'd have gotten more," was all he said. "Keep doing your saline flushes and come back and see me in two weeks." I went home and continued to ingratiate myself into my new squadron, VT-3.

I'd finished the Ground School phase and was still looking for medical clearance to begin flying. My plan,

[4] NAMI Naval Aerospace Medical Institute

nearly full proof in my estimation, had one glaring omission, an up-chit (medical flight clearance).

Meanwhile, Sherri was gainfully employed as a receptionist/office manager at a small law firm. It didn't take long for my lovely bride to question the wisdom of hitching her wagon to my grand scheme. While she was toiling away, I began a regime of morning study followed by an afternoon of catching up on old movies. At day's end, she would often catch me heading down the backstairs with the garbage as I completed the few domestic chores I'd intended to tackle that day.

I had two more appointments with Dr. Mengele prior to Christmas. At each, that pesky cloudiness was still evident in my x-rays.

For the holidays, we trekked home to Iowa. We decided to rent a car and drive because flying was deemed a risk for my still suspect noggin. I recall driving straight through—seventeen hours—the last half of our journey in a blizzard.

At Christmas, I recall going to midnight mass to celebrate the incarnation of our Lord but mostly to show off in my dress blues. It was an early example of my tangential relationship with God.

Out of the blue, my father announced one day at the local eatery—to townsfolk who had asked after me—that I was in flight school and that I was going to be an F-14 fighter pilot. Somewhat embarrassed by this brazen pronouncement, I chided him for this presumptive attitude while secretly appreciating his confidence in me. That said, looking ahead to all the obstacles I still faced, I chalked Dad's statement up to blissful ignorance. There were a lot of obstacles yet on the road to any horizon so bright. I hadn't even been cleared to fly. There was, at this juncture, no clear path for me to reach the nirvana that had me flying Tomcats. Yet, despite the realities of the situation, I remained sanguine about my prospects for the future as we headed south.

Back in Pensacola, we quickly fell into our respective routines. You've heard of "gym rats?" Well, I became a "squadron rat." Every morning I'd drive up to Whiting Field from our home near Escambia Bay. Once there, I'd hang around the ready room for a bit, go out to the flight line and practice my preflight of the T-34C Turbo-Mentor (the airplane then used in primary flight school to train all prospective Naval Aviators). After that, I'd head over to the academic building to study the procedures of each syllabus hop.

You've heard people ask, "Where were you when?" On January 28th, 1986, I was studying in the academic building of NAS Whiting Field when the officer of the deck came rushing in to turn on CNN. I knew it had to be something big. It was. I saw the huge white plume and remnants of the Challenger (space shuttle) shooting across an azure sky.

A tragedy, to be certain, but I was concerned with my own issues. At this stage of my life, I chalked my infantile level of empathy up to an admirable sense of mission, a laser focus on the future I envisioned.

Every weekday I did a preflight, studied the primary syllabus, generally ingratiated myself with my squadron mates, did my Water Pik (nasal irrigation), and awaited my next medical evaluation. At my next medical appointment, Dr. Mengele suggested a more drastic approach was indicated.

"What we could try is called a 'nasal antral window.' See, the cloudiness on your x-ray isn't clearing up. You are still doing your nasal flushes, right?"

I nodded, trying to imagine how nasal antral windows could be more drastic than weekly x-rays of my skull, not to mention getting stabbed in the face with a huge needle.

"What I'm suggesting will work. The question is, how badly you want to fly?"

"If it'll work, let's do it, sir."

"First, don't you want to know what it is?"

I'd run hundreds of miles, done thousands of push-ups, tore my anterior cruciate ligament, and decided, on more than one occasion, that drowning was preferable to failure. Dr. Mengele could have told me that the first step in the procedure involved removing your left testicle, and my response would have been, "sign me up."

Fortunately, a nasal antral window isn't that aggressive. The best way to think of it, at least in my pea-sized brain, is that the left and right maxillary sinus cavities are connected when a large hole or "window" is opened between the two. Of course, the two are connected already. A window would simply enlarge the hole that already exists; this would allow pressure to equalize more readily, presumably preventing the issue that had, at this point, rendered me "med down" for nearly four months.

"Think about it, talk to your spouse and get back to me with your answer when we see you next week."

I was still operating—at least on the outside—as though everything was fine. Inside, however, I'd begun to worry a bit. The inkling of something dark and sinister lurking in the shadowy periphery of my mind had just started to claw its way to the surface of my psyche. I wondered if I'd ever get the opportunity to be an aviator.

A week later, after irradiating my skull, Dr. Mengele asked me about the surgery he had proposed.

"The x-rays still show that cloudiness at the bottom of your left maxillary sinus. So, while your sinuses are mostly clear, I cannot, in good conscience, write you an up chit. You have a choice; you can call it quits. After all, you've gone through. There'd be no shame in it."

As he was saying this, I was totally poker-faced, but inside I was screaming NOOOO! While I watched my career flash before my eyes, Dr. Mengele continued.

"The other possibility is we could try the nasal antral window that I mentioned last week."

I nodded.

"Let's do it," I said.

I remember that the gurney squeaked as they wheeled me down the long hall toward surgery. It was early February. I'd been med down (in a non-flying status) since early September. Since then, I'd been commissioned as an Ensign in the United States Naval Reserve, mostly memorized the entire Primary Flight Syllabus, and caught up on nearly every old movie that existed.

Sherri gave me a kiss and the doors closed. I don't recall if I said a prayer or not, but I'm sure if I did, it wasn't that I would come out of the surgery safely; it was probably something to the effect, "God, I hope this works."

The plan was that I would wait two to four weeks before I could start in with the water pik again. After a month or two of self-administered nasal irrigation, there would be a final board to evaluate my status, either allowing me to commence flying or end my embryonic career.

Time marches on. Had I to do it over again, we would have worried less and enjoyed Florida more. For instance, that fall, a local kid at Pensacola High had shredded the record books. People kept saying you should go catch a game. We never did. I think the first time I ever saw Emmet Smith run was on television when he was a Cowboy. The other thing that pains me is that we never made it down to the happiest place on earth, and we never went to Epcot. I didn't work for nearly a year, but taking time to smell the roses? In Pensacola, we never fully did.

That's because my career and consequently our chosen path in life hung on the recommendation, the rather capricious opinion, of one man. In late April, I finally got clearance from a panel of physicians. Final approval, though, or at least the end to my persecution, came a week later when Dr. Mengele—the head of ENT at NAMI—would decide whether or not to let me continue. Note to self and the reader: we were never on "our chosen path?" Sherri, even way back then, was a truly patient and virtuous woman. No, when I say "our chosen path," what I really mean is "*my* chosen path." Back then, the depths of my selfishness were tremendous.

The morning of my appointment, for the first time in my life, I got down on my knees at the foot of our bed and prayed for deliverance. I prayed to God that my dream of flying jets would not end on this day for a reason as ignominious as sinusitis. I prayed that I would get my UP CHIT and be allowed to start flying.

Dr. Mengele gave me a thorough examination and then sent me for one last round of x-rays. Upon my return, he reviewed the films and didn't say anything for a long time. All the while, I remained stoic, but of course, I was dying inside. With a word, my dreams of being a carrier-based fighter pilot could end. Then it came.

"Honestly, your sinuses seem completely clear, but for some time now, your left maxillary sinus has shown a cloudiness that in all good conscience prevents me from clearing you for jets. I'm willing to grant you a conditional clearance, allowing you to start flying on a medical waiver and notating on your records that I'm recommending you for helicopters or P-3s[5] only."

My mind raced. My career was running down my leg because I walked into the altitude chamber with a cold. I wanted to fly pointy-nosed go fasts from ships. In no way had I gone through all I'd been through to fly helicopters. I'm screaming inside, but with my best poker face, I replied, "Okay, Sir, but if it'll save you any

[5] The P-3 was a large land-based multi-engined turboprop used for surveillance and Anti-Submarine Warfare.

time, I'm married. I don't want to go to sea. I want P-3s anyhow. It's my first choice."

I won that hand. The pot was the largest I've ever been in. Dr. Mengele never recommended me for P-3s or helos. He simply gave me a conditional up chit.

Fam One (familiarization hop one) is simply meeting your instructor followed by a preflight evolution. You learn how to strap in, and that's it. So, here's the deal. Most students graduate from AOCS on Friday and start ground school on Monday. They finish ground school on a Friday and start with Fam One on Monday. Indeed, becoming a Naval Aviator is like taking a sip of water from a fire hose.

Recall that I'd spent several months memorizing the entire syllabus while med down. On Fam One, I was giving my instructor tips on the preflight. Like an idiot, I told him that I'd been med down for several months. Fortunately, I don't think my confession registered. After Fam One, the USMC Captain who became my first flight instructor figured that his student was a genius.

Once I got my up chit, I loosened up a bit. On weekends we took up sailing. Real Naval Officers must learn the tradition and skill of sailing. In aviation officer candidate school (AOCS), we were given a class on it. Interestingly if one understands the mechanics of sailing, they will also have a rudimentary grasp of aerodynamics.

Yet it was the swashbuckling adventure of a nautical jaunt, even if it was just around the Naval Air

Station's tiny marina in a Sunfish, that had me humming Buffett. Perhaps it was my unhealthy obsession with Camelot that left me imagining myself at the tiller of Victura.[6] Certainly, someone who'd had an intensive week-long course on sailing, despite growing up seventeen hundred miles from the nearest ocean, would have all the details necessary to master the skill.

On our maiden voyage, I rigged the sunfish on a tiny beach while Sherri staged our gear. The assembly went well. Sherri, back with the gear, watched my workman-like precision. After a few minutes, we were loading the craft and would soon shove off.

It was a beautiful day. Puffy little cumulus clouds marched across a painfully blue May sky. I made one last cursory search of the bag that had once contained the mainsail and other accoutrements of a rental sunfish and, to my surprise, found a small plug.

I spent the next several minutes looking for a hole in which this plug was to fit. I went up to the main office of the MWR[7] facility to ask, but there was a large line forming and only one sailor behind the counter. I went back to the craft. This had not been in any of my classes on sailing. Daylight was burning. Finally, I said to Sherri, "I don't see where this plug goes. It's probably a spare," I said, tossing it into the bottom of the boat. Then we shoved off.

We sailed for several hours. We went out to a little spit of land where we enjoyed a simple picnic. Sherri, I'm sure, was duly impressed by my seamanship. It was very romantic. It had been a great day so far.

---

[6] Victura was John F. Kennedy's sailboat. It was given to him by his father on his fifteenth birthday. He loved sailing it for the remainder of his life.

[7] MWR – Morale Welfare and Recreation promotes and maintains all leisure time activities for soldiers and sailors.

Tacking against the wind on our way back to the marina, I noted that our little boat was behaving rather sluggishly. I looked at other sunfish sailing nearby and noted that the other boats were riding much higher in the water.

Long story short, that plug was, in fact, quite important. To which anyone with any sense might respond, "no shit."

The good news is that Sunfish sailboats can't be sunk. On that day, I proved this fact once again. Some genius, right?

By Fam Six, my instructor still considered me a genius. However, my flying skills were proving to be less than stellar. After five flights of pranging airplanes on runways in the area, it was obvious that I'd yet to master the concept of flaring to land. I couldn't see it. I'd flare too early, stall the aircraft, and then come down like a ton of shit. Or I'd flare too late, i.e., not at all, and land hard. We had to report at least one hard landing after each of my first five hops.

The problem was that Fam Seven was to be my first solo. That meant that on Fam Six, I had to master landing the T-34C. Unless I could demonstrate an ability to land safely, I'd fail Fam Six.

Like learning to drown-proof and tread water, landing came with a sudden obvious "aha moment." I, for whatever reason, could not picture the proper flare-to-land technique in order to touch down gently. Never mind that most of my future landings would not require such delicacy. Prior to thousands of practice carrier landings, one must first learn the subtle, though less precise, method of flaring to land.

On Fam Six, I was flying with my Secondary On-Wing Instructor. I don't know this for sure, but I'm guessing that my Primary Instructor had by now given up on me as my stick and rudder skills were proving less than stellar. On the sixth or seventh trip around the pattern, my flight instructor had a very simple suggestion.

"On final, when you think it's time to flare, take about half of it out, evaluate, and then flare some more when it's really time."

With that sentence, I went from numerous flailing attempts at the mysterious concept of flaring to land to multiple successful demonstrations. I passed with flying colors.

My first solo, a true rite of passage, went off without a hitch, mostly. The philosophy of Naval Aviation is to begin by training Student Naval Aviators to fly VFR (under visual flight rules). As such, prospective aviators learn basic instruments such as those monitoring the engine, the attitude indicator, altimeter, and airspeed indicator. In other words, they teach you how to fly the airplane, but they don't teach you how to read the full instrument panel, at least right away.

I flew up to one of the practice fields to do some touch and goes. After several flawless landings, I flew around southern Alabama for a while until I deemed it time to RTB (return to base).

Southern Alabama is a sea of endless pine forests interrupted by the occasional patch of red dirt. After several minutes of mindlessly boring holes in the sky, it dawned on me that I was no longer in familiar territory. I became more anxious as I looked for any recognizable landmark. At some point, I had to admit that I was lost.

Any pilot nominally familiar with the instrument panel would have dialed up NAS Whiting on the TACAN[8] and flown home. Unfortunately, I'd yet to learn what a TACAN was. After some time, I spied a town amid the endless pine forests. I dipped down to five hundred feet. As is the case with most towns in America, the town's name was emblazoned on the side of its water tower, Brewton, Alabama. I had to buzz the water tower, but now I knew my way home.

It was around this time that I first discovered my distinct disadvantage. Most of the other Student Naval Aviators, those seriously vying for jets, had prior flight time. Most of them had just enough flight time in non-retractable single-engine aircraft to solo. My thinking was their clear advantage had evaporated with my tour of Southern Alabama. Another way to say it is "ignorance is bliss."

In my mind, I was right where I wanted to be. From a grade standpoint, despite my previous issues landing the Turbo Mentor, I was sitting pretty. My plans were working precisely as envisioned.

Sherri and I spent weekends sailing with our friends and neighbors. Once I'd mastered the Sunfish and the plug, I quickly graduated to bigger boats. With the benefit of hindsight, oblivious and ignorant is the way I'd describe myself in those days. I continued to wow my instructor with my perceived eidetic grasp of the

---

[8] TACAN - A tactical air navigation system, commonly referred to by the acronym TACAN, is a navigation system used by military aircraft. It provides the user with bearing and distance (slant-range) to a ground or ship-borne station. It is a more accurate version of the VOR/DME system that provides bearing and range information for civil aviation.

procedures. The grade point for getting jets in those days—if you were Navy—was around three point zero three. At the end of fams (Familiarization Syllabus), I was sitting around three point zero six.

Chapter Ten:
Jets

We were young, and we were foolish. The possibility that our destiny was not preordained did not occur to us. You would think that after all I'd been through, our tenuous grasp of an impossible dream would have been self-evident, yet I was certain, so certain, that jets were my manifest destiny.

Sherri and I bought shrimp on the docks. We picnicked on the beach and spent weekends sailing.

After fam (Familiarization), we started Radio Instrument (RI) training. This is where students learned to fly in instrument conditions. In the goo. It entailed flight time under the hood, a device that could be pulled up along the canopy to totally impede one's ability to see outside the cockpit. We flew for hours in the simulator. Students call it the mushroom factory because blackness reigns. It wasn't long before I was intimately familiar with all instruments on the instrument panel. Despite my confidence, it was soon evident that my skills as an IFR (Instrument Flight Rules) flyer were not impressive. My grades began going down.

Fortunately, the clock ran out before my grades trended below jet grades. I ended my time in the T-34 with just over sixty-seven hours of flight time and a three point zero four grade point average. Had I been a Marine, I would have flown helicopters. Back then, you had to have a three point zero six or eight for jets in the USMC, only a three point zero three to fly Navy. Can you say, "skin of your teeth?" Now we were moving to Kingsville, Texas. There I'd begin training in jets.

Sherri and I trekked across I-10 along the Gulf Coast in our tight-knit, two-vehicle caravan. She had her first Hurricane on Bourbon Street. We spent a night in the French Quarter. We thought we were going west but eventually found ourselves about four hours south of Houston in the town of Kingsville, in those days, the largest Navy jet training base.

I flew the T-2C Buckeye, a straight-winged, two-engine, tandem-seat trainer jet, affectionately referred to as the "guppy."

Everything happens quicker in a jet. In a jet, turns are bigger, happen sooner, and require prior planning. It was the first time I heard the words "you're behind the airplane."

We spent six weeks on a detachment in Key West. There, despite my general lack of innate "stick and rudder skills," I learned to fly formation. It wasn't pretty like treading water and flaring to land. The keys to this mysterious skill were discovered suddenly and in the nick of time. I became minimally proficient on the fourteenth of fifteen formation flights. Prior to that, I was certain that my time in jets would end suddenly in a fireball at fifteen to twenty-thousand feet. My instructors would show me the picture, putting the jet in perfect formation, and then shake the stick and say, "okay, you've got the aircraft," to which the student (me) answered, "I've got it." The jet was, for a few seconds, rock solid in formation, and then slowly, but with ever-increasing amplitude, the variations would grow until the proximity of two aircraft sharing the same piece of sky became a clear and present danger. At which point, to avoid swapping paint, I'd fall out of formation.

Then, like the airplane had a memory, the instructor would put us right back in position, and we'd do it again and again and again.

Nearing the end of our go-juice, one of my favorite instructors would save enough gas for an impromptu low level. I remember screaming past a sailboat anchored in an emerald bay near marathon key, a topless woman waving enthusiastically from the deck as we pulled vertical. We'd chase clouds for a bit and then RTB[9] to NAS Key West, where we'd park on the Blackbirds[10] flight line.

After debriefing, we'd go out for dinner and repair to some local watering hole. Fighter pilots are larger than life, and the stories of outrageous behavior that I've seen, or sadly, been a part of, could fill this book. And so, you end up with a bunch of wannabes trying to top one another's outrageous behavior. The earliest indication of wild behavior that I can recall is when I saw a guy try to climb a utility pole on Duvall street after a night of drunken revelry at Sloppy Joe's. He ended up

---

9 RTB is Return(ed) To Base.

10 VF-45, the "Blackbirds," was an adversary squadron operating out of NAS Key West from 1963-1996.

flat on his back on the sidewalk, moaning in pain after a nasty fall. He spent the rest of the det (detachment) trying to hide his injuries so he could stay with our class. Compared to what was to come over the next several years, this was tame stuff.

As per normal, my performance was average. In the T-2C, no one thought me a genius anymore. I had not had months to memorize the syllabus. My stick and rudder skills were not bad, nor were they particularly good.

Yet my long-range plan remained intact. We had initially set up camp on the south side of town in a sad little rental apartment. Two months into our six-month lease, we managed to negotiate an early exit and moved to base housing. There, Sherri's lonely existence took a positive turn. We met neighbors, all of whom were Student Naval Aviators and their young brides. Figuratively, we were all in the same boat.

Bachelors were housed in the BOQ (Bachelor Officers' Quarters). Young married couples were a minority when it came to Students. The remainder of base housing residents were comprised of instructor pilots or officers—and their families—filling other billets.

I mentioned my favorite instructor a few paragraphs earlier. Captain Cresh, USMC, possessed movie star good looks and happily flaunted a jet-black mane that grossly exceeded the typical high and tight of the Corps. He smoked a big cigar when out on the town.

He was everything I imagined a fighter pilot should be. Late in the syllabus, I found out he flew helicopters.

The only real fighter pilot in our squadron was our skipper, Captain "Buck" Rogers, USN. I was three-quarters of the way through Intermediate Jets when he and I, both a few drinks into a party, first exchanged pleasantries. The movie "Top Gun" had come out earlier that year. Like most of my contemporaries in primary flight school, I had seen the movie multiple times. I vaguely recall asking the skipper if you could really do that in a Tomcat? I had asked him about a line in the movie where "Maverick" tells "Goose" that he intends to "put on the brakes and he'll fly right by," or words to that effect. Today, I cringe at the inherent stupidity of this question, but despite my obvious naiveté, my C.O. simply smiled and answered, "Well, sort of."

Of course, the end of my time as a Guppy Driver coincided with the thing that separates a Naval Aviator from all other pilots. Carrier Qualification. We spent weeks practicing simulated carrier landings on the field. When the day finally came, I remember that the experience happened quickly, and I spent most of it in a fog of confusion. My first carrier landing aboard the USS Lexington was anticlimactic. I flew down to a centered ball, three-wire. If memory serves, it was a fair pass. Note: Pilots are graded on a four-point scale throughout their careers.[11] Every time they land on a ship, a grade is given. An "okay" is a four-point-zero, a "fair' is a three, a no-grade is a two, and a rare "cut" pass is a one-point-zero. At any rate, my first shipboard landing wasn't a big deal. I do recall that it felt weird, harder, less

---

[11] Landing grades are in fact based on a five-point scale – from lowest to highest – 1 is a "cut," 2 is a "no grade," 3 "fair," 4 "okay," and 5 is "okay underlined," which I have never seen or heard of anyone getting. Hence, it is effectively a four-point scale.

forgiving perhaps, landing on the steel deck with carrier-pressurized tires.

After landing came the truly frightening part of the evolution, taxiing on the crowded flight deck. That was followed a few seconds later by my first cat shot. The catapult launches you with enough speed to go flying once you are shot off the pointy end. That requires about four G's of acceleration. The T-2C had this thing called the "Cat Grip." It folded down near the throttle, and the pilot was supposed to wrap his hand around it as well as the throttles to avoid going to idle when experiencing the g-force of a catapult shot. There was a large sign in bold letters on a large open hatch between catapults one and two. It read, "CAT GRIP!" To this day, I can see that sign clearly in my mind's eye. Yet, the entire evolution was a blur. As I saluted the catapult officer, I felt like I was forgetting something. I was reminded a few seconds later when over water, at idle, the Air Boss screaming into my headset, I shoved the throttles forward. Despite the initial excitement, my remaining passes went well.

My plan was beginning to coalesce. I could see the future, or so I thought, and it was so bright it reminded me of Timbuk3.[12]

Yet, the reality was that despite graduating to advanced jets and flying another new airplane—the Douglas TA-4J Skyhawk—my days as a perceived genius were but a distant memory. Moreover, my stick and rudder skills were only slightly above average.

---

[12] 1986 Rock and Roll song "The Future's So Bright, I Gotta Wear Shades" by Timbuk3.

The Skyhawk is a tall, tight-fitting, narrow-footed airplane. A sharp turn on the closely spaced tricycle gear could result in putting the jet on its side. The cockpit is so small it feels as though you strap the jet on to go flying. It's still not quite the fighter that we dreamed of, but variants were widely used in Vietnam. Even the training version felt tactical. The airplane wasn't supersonic, but the little delta-winged aircraft had the best roll rate of any airplane I ever flew.

I struggled through each phase of the syllabus. I flew with Rambo, who tried to teach me the intricacies of Instrument Flying in the airplane. Rambo never got to fly fighters. I heard that she became a COD driver (carrier onboard delivery) in the fleet. That was back in the days before women could legally fly combat aircraft.

Sherri and I made good friends, and though our future was far from certain, I considered it a foregone conclusion. As such, we finally exhaled, just a bit, and made the most of our stay in south Texas. We visited relatives living in Corpus Christi. I remember one visit up to Corpus during the fall harvest. It was a bit windy that day and the loose cotton blew across the road like snow.

Corpus was great. We ate seafood at Snoopy's down on the beach, drank beer, and listened to Jimmy Buffett.

Back in Kingsville, I hunted in my spare time. Birds mostly, doves and ducks, though I did chase whitetails and javelina unsuccessfully on more than one occasion.

We became expert judges of Tex-Mex and aficionados of Texas-style barbeque. And, to this day, the most exciting football game I've ever seen was at Texas A & I University.

I had a deal with folks in scheduling. In the fall, they never scheduled me before ten am. I would hunt ducks with my new dog, a Golden Retriever named Aileron, out on Baffin Bay.

We got Aily up in Corpus. Sherri and I accompanied our neighbors and good friends—the Cooks. We were just along for the ride, or so I thought. We came home with two puppies that day. Aileron's sister Gemini grew up at the Cook residence.

Class began the next day. Aileron was trained according to Richard A. Wolters's "Gun Dog" methodology. He was not the best hunting dog that ever lived, but he was well trained and disciplined and very smart. Most importantly, he was a beloved pet.

I cannot recall the order of the syllabus with certainty. I think it was Road Recce, Air to Ground, then ACM (Air Combat Maneuvering). The order doesn't matter. I do recall that all three segments were fun. It was just a taste of what would happen regularly in tactical jets. I'd made it through most of the syllabus relatively unscathed. I wasn't exactly lighting the world on fire. My grades, like most of my life, were average at best. Road Recce was a syllabus that introduced you to low-level navigation and simulated attacks. If memory serves, my grades were slightly above average in this phase.

It was followed by the Air to Ground phase. We dropped practice bombs, and while I never embarrassed myself by doing something stupid or dangerous, my grades were below average. It was on one of these hops that I saw my one and only NAFOD. A NAFOD is the worst grade that a student aviator can get. It results in immediate expulsion from the program. One of the other guys in my division (four-ship) crossed under three other airplanes carrying bombs. NAFOD stands for No Apparent Fear of Death. After the debrief, I never saw that guy again.

At this stage, students were starting to talk about selections. Of course, the "needs of the Navy" would ultimately determine what jet a guy flew. That said, the Navy considered a person's selections—I believe we got four—as well as their success in various stages of the syllabus. So, at this point, I wondered what I'd end up with. Thus far, I'd not distinguished myself in any phase of advanced jets.

Then we started ACM. We flew basic aerobatics and did some very rudimentary BFM (basic fighter maneuvers) and one vs. one simulated combat.

Since I'd started flying airplanes, none of my instructors had ever been wowed by my innate abilities. I was a likeable guy, and I hadn't gotten noticed for being scary or dangerous, but ACM was different. It was like athletics in the sky. In a real dogfight, you win, or you die. That imparts a level of intensity to every simulated encounter and renders other contests pedantic. That sort of ultimate competition seemed right to me. I finally found something I was good at.

Instructors must have talked about it, this lackluster student who'd done nothing remarkable suddenly performing as an accomplished aviator. I'm not sure if those discussions ever happened, but I did notice that instructors were suddenly treating me differently. During all of flight school, my goal had been to remain somewhat anonymous. To sort of fly under the radar, as it were. Famous students didn't hang around long. They usually got famous because they had a penchant for doing something stupid or dangerous. Don't get me wrong, Naval Aviators are signing up for danger whenever they leave terra firma, but instructors are there to ensure that would-be aviators manage and minimize risk throughout the mission.

Now, though, people knew me for the right reasons. I was quite pleased. My plan for world domination was proceeding on course. Not only was I good at Air Combat Maneuvering -for a Student Naval Aviator at least—but I had developed a reputation for being easy to work with. I flew whenever and wherever the schedules writers penciled me in. I did a cross-country flight to San Diego. My first time there. Happily, my first real landing in El Paso, Texas—an intermediate pitstop for gas—was uneventful. I didn't crash as I once had in the simulator.

Things were going great. I started looking forward to Carrier Qualification. That is when I faced my second bout of sinusitis. I was med-down again. The go-to mix for me would be Ampicillin and Sudafed. Now that I'm older and wiser, I sometimes wonder if Captain Mengele might have been right to recommend that I fly P-3s or Helos. Thank God he never put it in writing.

The class I'd started with went to the boat and got winged. I watched. Instructors started suggesting callsigns for people as they got close to earning their wings. Initially, folks wanted me to be Geezer. My last name is Geneser (Jen-ee-zer). I'd been med down with sinusitis for a couple of weeks. Eventually, I was dubbed Sneezer. Not only was it appropriate, but it also rhymed. It could be worse. To this day, there are people who would not know my name. They only know me by my callsign.

When I was finally med-up again, it was late fall. By the time I flew out to Lady Lex (USS Lexington, CVT-16) steaming somewhere south of the Dry Tortugas, it was early December. While there (Key West), I went snorkeling for the first time in my life. I was mesmerized by the rich and colorful world existing just below the surface.

Most importantly, other than a blown tire upon one of my landings, I do not recall carrier quals (carrier qualification) in advanced jets as being particularly eventful. Of course, I suppose describing landing on a ship as uneventful is a bit of an understatement.

On December 17th of 1987, exactly eighty-four years after Orville and Wilbur flipped a coin to see who would go first, I received my "wings of gold." It had taken two years and three months to reach this milestone. My dad and father-in-law attended the ceremony. They had made the seventeen-hundred-mile trip to witness the event, driving straight down I-35.

I recall dinner with our neighbors, as we'd gotten winged on the same day. They had invited a family friend, a Navy Captain, who'd flown an A-7 in the Libya raid there to help us celebrate. He arrived with nary a moment to spare, flying a two-seat A-7. At dinner, he regaled us with his stories. I was thoroughly enthralled as I imagined our future. It was truly a night to remember. Eight of us had gotten winged that afternoon. As luck would have it, our class was caught up in a fighter draft. Three guys got F/A-18 Hornets, two Navy, and one Marine. Another Marine got AV-8B Harriers, one Navy guy got A-6 Intruders, and three of us got F-14s.

Chapter Eleven:
Gunfighter

While home on leave, we got word that we were going to the west coast Naval Air Station Miramar, Fighter Town USA, San Diego, CA. I would commence training in VF-124—the Gunfighters—in the F-14 Tomcat.

Note that the military designation of airplanes, and therefore, that of all U.S. Navy aircraft and the squadrons in which they operate, have a general naming convention. So that we're all on the same page, the letter "T" is for "training." The letter "V" stands for "fixed-wing," and "H" is "helicopter." One would think that "F" would be "fixed-wing," but that would be incorrect. That's because "F" stands for "fighter."

For instance, while I was in the training command, I served in VT-3 and flew the T-34. In intermediate jets, I flew the T-2C in VT-23. In advanced jets, I was in VT-21 and flew the TA-4J. "A," by the way, stands for "attack."

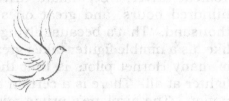

Now I reported to VF-124, where I'd learn to fly the F-14 Tomcat. I could legitimately call myself a fighter pilot. Well, sort of, anyway. I most certainly would not make such a bold statement in front of any experienced Tomcat driver. Legitimate drivers have at least five hundred hours, and great ones have more than one thousand. That's because flying such a large airplane like it's a nimble fighter takes great skill. The argument of many Hornet pilots is that the Tomcat isn't truly a fighter at all. There is a certain amount of truth to the notion. The airplane's prime mission originally was to carry Phoenix missiles and shoot down Russian Hordes attacking the ship from beyond visual range (BVR). Yet, nobody ever told Naval Aviators that the airplane was only meant to be an Interceptor. The best fighter guys in the Navy lived in San Diego, and they flew great big airplanes that had the most powerful radar on earth.

My first trip down the runway in an airplane that was as heavy as a fully loaded B-17 (of WWII fame) felt like I was driving a cement truck, albeit a fast one. Of course, once you're wheels-in-the-well, the jet handles beautifully, at speed anyway. I broke the sound barrier for the first time on my first flight in a Tomcat.

To this day, though I would end my career as a Hornet guy, I consider the F-14 Tomcat the most beautiful airplane ever to grace the heavens. That said, it did have some issues. It was not my favorite airplane to fly.

I was in the West Coast FRS (Fleet Replacement Squadron). As per normal, my grades were nothing to write home about. That said, I held my own. I didn't get a new callsign or anything. Typically, if you did something really dumb, you might, because of your ineptitude, earn a new callsign. Usually, a new moniker tended to be not so subtly derogatory.

I quickly discerned that getting a sip from the firehose of Naval Air training had not ended with my winging. Wings just marked, as Winston Churchill once said of the second battle of El Alamein, "the end of the beginning." I would learn and get better every day. I had trouble with aerial tanking. I got it done, but it wasn't pretty. I dreaded the prospect each time for years.

The reasons were multiple. Naval Aviators don't get plugged like the Air Force. A boom operator doesn't fly a coupling device down to some fuel receptacle on your aircraft. In the Navy, we extend a probe and then fly that probe into a basket at the end of a fuel hose trailing the tanker. The coupling device is at the bottom of that cone-shaped basket. In combat, this procedure is totally silent, but sometimes in peacetime, the Pilot, RIO, or BN[13] will announce that they're "plugged and receiving." At any rate, my first time tanking ended with a small piece of my probe door breaking off. Fortunately, that chunk of metal missed the intake of my right engine. My first tanking experience ended with my first "provisional down."

My next attempt went better. Nothing was broken, and after several successful plugs, I was deemed a "qual."

As had become my modus operandi, my skill level as a Tomcat driver did not "wow" anyone. That said, I was always in the hunt. No one considered me a virtuoso. Yet, more importantly, no one considered me a danger. I was "steady Eddie." "Joe Average."

Unlike most of my fellow students, I had a wife. Moreover, she was pregnant. We had been trying, or at least forgoing any precautions, since our wedding day. For more than three years, nothing. We had only been in San Diego for a few weeks when Sherri announced her pregnancy.

Meanwhile, fighting the Tomcat centered around the AWG-9 radar, the Phoenix missile, and BVR (beyond visual range) engagement. The airplane was originally

---

[13] BN – Bombardier Navigator, RIO is Radar Intercept Officer

developed to combat Soviet bombers. Backfires armed with air-launched cruise missiles marshaling somewhere over the horizon to attack a battle group and, ideally, sink an aircraft carrier. Tomcats would range far from the carrier and provide an opposing barrier. The hope was that such a gauntlet would make the calculus of an attack too costly. This Clanceyesk scenario was, though unlikely, the one we were training to combat. Though no one knew it then, we were operating near the end of the cold war era. History tells us that we tend to train for the last war. In retrospect, the airplane and its mission, despite being new to me, were on the verge of extinction.

It was not all work and no play. Naval Aviators, particularly fighter guys, are notoriously high speed, low drag, louder, flashier, outrageous by any metric. As a member of this group, I considered it my solemn duty to help perpetuate the stereotype.

While Sherri endured pregnancy, I was busy doing happy hour at the officer's club. Wednesday night was lady's night. In those days, large numbers of beautiful young girls flocked to Miramar to dance and imbibe and perhaps snare a fighter pilot. Most fighter guys at Miramar would show up. For guys looking to score, it was a virtual shooting gallery, a SOCAL smorgasbord. If you wore a flight suit and could fog a mirror, your chances for a hookup were extremely likely.

I know what you're thinking because I'm thinking it too. What an asshole. Stay with me, though. In those days, I had two things to help me from crossing any line of moral turpitude. First, I took my marriage vows seriously. Secondly, my commute was forty-five minutes, and despite skirting dangerously close to occasions of sin at least three nights a week, my looming commute prevented me from getting stupid drunk. Thus I managed to retain some level of inhibition.

I was convinced that I had achieved a level of debauchery in college bordering on virtuosity—silly me. I would spend the next decade proving time and again what an amateur I'd been. My descent into wretchedness would be gradual, nearly imperceptible, but it was consistent.

Meanwhile, the days of mastering the Tomcat continued. I should probably mention that folks just leaving the FRS do not achieve anything close to mastery. To become a true master in the F-14 takes several years and several million dollars. People just leaving the Fleet Replacement Squadron are, at best, apprentices. As I considered my prospects, I began to understand that while earning my wings was an accomplishment, doing so was like moving from junior high to high school.

Still, at this stage of my career, I understood that the inherent danger of Naval Aviation required a modicum of bravery. Although that is true to a degree, public perception vastly outstrips reality. Fighter Pilots are not fearless. They simply don't let fear rule them. They are, in fact, sometimes scared shitless, but instead of saying "I'll never do that again," like most sane people, they go out and do it time and again.

This strange brew is like a drug. The adrenaline fix becomes dangerous when it comes to rule one's thought process. Happily, for American taxpayers, in my career, I have never met an individual where the rush of impending death exceeded logical risk parameters. That mental calculus keeps an inherently risky profession, if not totally safe, at least within the bounds of reason. It is always a balancing act. Fighter pilots, good ones, are always operating on the very edge.

Discovery of where that "edge" happens to be is something aviators will eventually figure out. Sadly, the folks that do not discover it in time often become "smoking holes in the ground."

It's an unforgiving business. Though not nearly so dangerous as it once was. A steep learning curve heightens one's odds of survival. In case you haven't figured it out already, my learning curve, though positive, could never be described as steep.

Nicholas, our first, entered the world on January 8th, a full six weeks ahead of schedule. Born in Poway, CA, he was soon transferred to San Diego's Children's hospital because they had a Neonatal Intensive Care Unit. The first time I saw my son, I thought he looked like a little frog. He was lying on his stomach, with his tiny, bowed legs splayed behind him. His posture invoked that of a green amphibian. As I marveled at my son, I wondered what his life would entail. The anticipation of a world of possibility lay before him. His first steps, first haircut, first day of school, first touchdown, first home run; my son was only a few hours old, and I had already imagined the smile on his face when he stood lakeside and proudly held up his first fish. In that instant, I knew that God was real, and I said a quick prayer of thanks.

After Nick was settled, I hauled ass back up Interstate Fifteen to the hospital in Poway. His mother was recovering from an emergency Cesarean after suffering Placentae Abruption, which happens when the placental lining has separated from the uterus of the mother prior to delivery. Doctors later told me that if it had been twenty or thirty years earlier, it's unlikely that either mother or child would have survived. I had dithered for more than an hour while Sherri bled profusely before calling the ambulance. It was our friend and neighbor, Mary, Nick's eventual Godmother, who finally convinced me to act. That night, for the second time in my life, I hit my knees.

This momentous event might have caused a less focused individual to take pause and consider the trajectory of one's life and examine the focus of one's priorities. Yet, I was supremely focused on the goal. Thoroughly indoctrinated in the extreme level of compartmentalization that Naval Aviation demands, in only a few days, I was flying once again.

Life has a way of diverting one's passions. For the first time in my life, I lost sight of my master plan. I forgot, for a time, my political ambitions, my quest to achieve. Instead, I only wanted to get to the fleet, to be a Tomcat driver, and, yes, be a good dad.

Much of the syllabus centered on BVR (Beyond Visual Range) engagements. In that world, the Tomcat was a very capable machine. Aside from its powerful radar, the airplane, with its complement of phoenix missiles, was capable of engaging multiple targets simultaneously. As such, the aircraft was indeed a formidable interceptor. In this role, however, success or failure depended mostly on the RIO (Radar Intercept Officer). Without a capable back-seater, the airplane was not especially useful.

Yet even though the weapons system was designed to carry thousand-pound missiles hundreds of miles and fire them well beyond the horizon at incoming Soviet bombers, the Navy had long considered the airplane as the service's preeminent fighter. Guys capable of wielding an airplane as heavy as a semi-tractor like it was the sword of a samurai warrior don't just fall from trees like ripened fruit. Extensive, intense, and purposeful training of body, mind, and soul is necessary. Total commitment, not unlike that of a Shotokan Karate sensei, is required. I had not sipped the Kool-Aid® just yet, but very soon, and for several years I would guzzle.

After six months of intensive training, the great equalizer, "the boat," was the final hurdle prior to us being turned loose in the fleet. Note: Naval Aviation does not turn one loose, ever. Intensive training ends only when you leave the Navy. The second thing I need to mention on behalf of all my Surface Warrior friends is that calling an Aircraft Carrier a "boat" is unforgivable.

That is why Aviators take every opportunity to refer to their ship (the carrier) as "the boat." Primarily it's simply a way to good-naturedly rib our "black shoe brothers." I know! Sisters, too! I was a Naval Officer long ago. This was before the Department of Defense was fully sexually integrated.

Before traveling down any number of rabbit holes that the previous paragraph may have opened—like why Surface Warfare Officers are referred to as "black shoes"—let me steer us back toward the point. My first carrier landing in a Tomcat was a fair pass. Unfortunately, it was also my best pass. I managed a smattering of fairs and no grades, but at the end of day one, it was determined that I wasn't quite ready for prime time. The thing that separates men from boys is night traps. My second "down." As a failure to qualify, I would get the opportunity to go through carrier qualifications again. Typically, Aviators get two attempts to prove that they're fleet material. A third opportunity isn't extended. People who can't wrestle the beast aboard are offered a chance to go through the program again—this time as a RIO (Radar Intercept Officer). I suppose my stomach was in knots, though looking back, I don't recall it as a particularly tense period. By then, I'd gotten used to having my back against the wall. I'd gotten a new RIO, and he, though an intense dude, had a calming effect on his pilot—i.e., me.

The Tomcat is a difficult airplane to fly on and off ships. Its engines had a notoriously slow spool-up time. Additionally, with the wings out, the airplane tended to float like a kite. I've heard people describe it as trying to balance on top of a beach ball. In an instant, you can go from floating on air to coming down hard like a ton of shit.

My second attempt at carrier qualification was a completely different experience. That's because of Guido. We'd gotten winged the same day, but in the West Coast Tomcat FRS, he was a class behind me. Consequently, when I disqualified on my first attempt at the ship, we wound up going to the boat together.

Guido is larger than life. Even then, everybody knew him. There are many reasons for this. First, he is an extreme extrovert among a very extroverted bunch. He's smart, funny, and fun-loving. He's a great stick, but he's also a good guy. He's rather small in stature, at about five feet four inches. He sat on a special pad to see over the instrument panel of the Tomcat when landing.

It was Guido's idea that led to our carrier qual class being dubbed "Los Banditos." He even had T-Shirts made for us all. I don't know. Looking back, it seems kind of corny. Yet there was a sense of comradery, a level of esprit de corps that developed. After that, all boat classes had nicknames and t-shirts.

After another month of bouncing and countless hours in the simulator, I soon found myself staring at the back of the ship again. Daytime landings went better, and this time I was deemed safe enough to try the night.

Bouncing is the euphemism for a circuit around the pattern where, on final approach, you "fly the ball" down to a touch-and-go. By the time I'd been allowed a second chance at carrier qualification in the Tomcat, I'd bounced thousands of times in three different airplanes.

However, on the night of my first night trap, I didn't realize that I would get to qualify many, many times. It's what carrier pilots do.

My first night trap was an "OK three-wire." After hundreds of night landings in the simulator, the automatic nature of my first real night trap was not a big deal. It wasn't all that dark, the seas were calm, and the wind was right down the angle deck. That first one seemed easy. I learned quickly that they wouldn't all be like that.

Chapter Twelve: Otis

Two of us were disqualified when I went to the boat the first time. My buddy Dozer and I had both managed to DQ on our first trip to the boat in Tomcats. Things were different on our second attempt. If my memory is correct, we were both in the top half of the "Los Banditos" class. I'm not sure, but Dozer may have finished second. Guido was Top Hook.

No surprise there. The surprise was that Dozer and I were sought by the VF-154 Black Knights. I suppose, in retrospect, this was a fairly astute strategy. Neither Dozer nor I had ever displayed anything that bordered on being dangerous. Furthermore, we'd both exhibited a degree of competency in our second respective trip to the boat. Perhaps the true stroke of genius was that by willingly falling on their collective swords with respect to choosing us two chuckleheads, they'd get better choices of RIOs (Radar Intercept Officers).

Recall that the Tomcat does its best work, beyond visual range, with its powerful radar and complement of

Phoenix missiles. That part of an engagement is run by the person in the backseat, i.e., the RIO.

In the late summer of 1989, we checked aboard as brand new Black Knights. Our compadres were sprinkled among other west coast Tomcat squadrons.

I think the first time we met Dozer and T, it was on account of our dogs. Aileron and Freckles played together in the park down near the kennels at NAS Miramar. They both stayed there for a time as we hunted for respective places to live. My sister often says, "God spelled backward," when describing our furry four-legged friends. On the day that we met Dozer and T, there was indeed some divine intervention at work. For more than half a decade, our lives were strangely and thankfully intertwined.

We had started at VF-124 together and went to the boat together twice. Dozer and I checked in to our new squadron on the same day. We would check out of the Black Knights, some three years and two months later, on the same day.

I titled this chapter "Otis" because the squadron's insignia and patch was a knight dressed in—you guessed it—black. Someone inevitably named him Otis in deference to Animal House, the movie, and the fictional "Otis and the Knights." I know. Fighter pilots are clever. I should briefly point out that today VFA-154 flies F/A-18Fs out of NAS Lemoore in California.

Recall that I'd spent much of my early life growing up in a lower-middle-class farming community. I'd never known a military officer. I'd grown up learning that in the military, one should not volunteer for anything. Going the extra mile to stand out was asking for trouble. I would spend the next few years of my life learning why this dictum was, for officers, exactly wrong. Furthermore, it's wrong for enlisted folks as well, at least in the peacetime Navy.

Additionally, recall that deep down, I harbor a tendency toward sloth. Couple this with the fact that by now, the moniker of genius, which I had enjoyed briefly in primary flight school, was now but a distant memory, and, well, I soon gravitated to my natural level. I was ranked last among junior officers.

I soon found myself back against the wall once again. It started the day I "saw the screws" for the first time in my life.

We were on NORPAC up near the Aleutian Islands. You know, the place where they film "Deadliest Catch." We were aboard CV-64, USS Constellation, CAG-14. I was chosen to accompany the Skipper and his wingman. We were the red force running a simulated attack on America's remote outpost, Shemya Air Force Base—the last US Island before Russia. The base closed as an Air Force base in 1994. It was evident that morning as we walked to our airplanes that it was going to be a varsity day. The sad fact was that we, Dozer and I, were the newest members of the J.V. After getting shot off the pointy end, we joined up overhead. Skipper was lead, Killer was Dash Two, and I was Dash Three. We pushed out west along the Aleutian chain. Halfway there, we rendezvoused with a USMC KC-130. I was first. Conservatively, with the erratic arctic wind, perhaps something not right with the aerodynamics of the basket, it was cycling up and down at least ten feet. I'd never seen such a thing. I'm pretty sure no one had. I tried to plug for several minutes, but with the basket moving twenty feet, it became apparent that I had a snowball's chance in hell of getting gas.

"If you don't get plugged in the next couple-a tries, let Killer give it a go," Skipper drawled. After chasing the basket for several minutes, I reluctantly slid out from behind the tanker and let Killer give it a try.

Killer was a senior JO (Junior Officer). He had completed two cruises and had more than one thousand hours in the Tomcat. Yet, it was soon evident that he, too, was going to have trouble getting gas. Meanwhile, time was ticking, and, with every mile, we got farther and farther from the ship. Killer tried and tried to plug the wildly gyrating basket, and, on perhaps his tenth or twelfth attempt, he succeeded.

Our Skipper—and flight lead—was next. He didn't have one thousand traps. He was still a cruise away from "cake in the ready room," but he did have several thousand hours in fighters and, as a former test pilot, had once been a finalist for astronaut selection. To say that he was a "good stick" would be a monumental understatement. Even he would need more than one attempt to get plugged. Again, it was a varsity day, but the Skipper defined varsity. He started getting gas after his second attempt. As he was finishing, he instructed us on how things would go.

"Killer, you and Sneezer head back to the ship, and I'll continue the simulated raid as a single." Of course, the implication was that we'd reached our "no gas range limit," and as a nugget (new guy), I could not find my ass with both hands, much less my way back to the boat without an experienced flight lead.

We turned back, me on Killer's wing. My RIO and I calculated how much gas we'd have when we crossed the ramp (landed).

My buddy Dozer had launched on that same cycle and would be returning on the same recovery. By the way, every commanding officer in the Navy, whether commanding a ship or not, is referred to as Skipper. So, when I tell you that our Skipper was on a double cycle—alone and unafraid on our simulated raid on Shemya—I'm referring to Black Knight One.

Meanwhile, Killer and I flew into the break. The carrier break—in the Air Force, they call it the Overhead—happens at six hundred feet. Recall that at the outset of this event, I'd immediately recognized, despite being a nugget, that it was a varsity day? The weather was dirty, with scud clouds at various levels.

The break is an aggressive turn to downwind. The more aggressive, the better, as it allows the airplane to bleed energy, i.e., slow down quickly. The practical considerations are that airplanes can quickly slow down to landing speed and get configured for touchdown. Consequently, more airplanes recover in less time. The result is that the carrier minimizes the time it spends turned into the wind. Yet, despite the fundamental reasons, Navy pilots dig the break because it's fun and it looks cool. Jets turning downwind, vaping like mad under heavy "G," go from four or five bills down to one-hundred and thirty knots in a matter of seconds.

All was well and good until I turned onto final. If you've flown a proper pattern, you roll out in the "groove" with fifteen seconds until touchdown. At first glance, I'd determined that things were amiss. The ship's attitude was alarming. It looked as though the ship were about to launch into the sky. The bow was high, and angry green water lapped near the ship's opening at the stern. I'd never seen anything like it.

"One-oh-three, Tomcat Ball, three point seven," my RIO said after I told him I had "the ball."

"Roger, Ball. Tomcat, axial winds fifty-four knots, MOVLAS.[14] ...Deck is down. You're on glideslope," the Landing Signal Officer said. The LSO, also known as "Paddles" on the radio, controls the position of the ball

---

[14] MOVLAS – The Manually Operated Visual Landing Aid System is typically used when the deck is pitching too fast or too much for the automated system to present true glideslope to the pilot.

and consequently the glideslope system manually whenever the water is big. On this day, the deck was moving plus or minus seventeen feet.

"Deck is down," the LSO said. No shit, I thought.

Then I saw something I only saw twice in my flying career. At about ten seconds, Paddles called, "deck is coming up." I was amazed at how much. At its apex, the ship looked like a giant submarine about to dive, and, for a second, I saw the ship's propellers come out of the water.

Of course, my eyes did not tarry. Staring at the back of the boat is a good way to die. The scan is quite simple: "meatball, lineup, angle of attack." This simple scan is a familiar mantra for anyone landing on a ship.

"Seeing the screws" is not something that happens every day. First, it must be daytime. You'd never see the ship's exposed propellers at night. Secondly, the weather must be extreme. On this day, the deck was moving a total of thirty-four feet. Most of the time, flight ops are canceled when the deck is pitching that much. Indeed, I was the last airplane to land. Airplanes still airborne were diverted to Adak Island.

As a "nugget," I flew with Tiger. He was a great RIO. Smart. Brave. He flew with me, so bravery was a requirement. Tiger's tactical acumen was beyond reproach. He came to the Black Knights from Top Gun, where he had been an instructor.

My flight lead was Spud. He's a Naval Academy grad and would eventually serve as Top Gun's Commanding Officer. In this graduate school of naval fighter aviation, primarily through osmosis, I would learn my trade well. It came at my usual glacial pace, but with time and patience, the ins and outs, the do's and don'ts of a Tomcat driver would someday flourish. While my skill level would marinate slowly and eventually lead me to become a better-than-average fighter guy, my first fleet tour was marred by a series of spectacular failures.

Most were self-induced. For instance, early on, I was a sponge soaking up all the knowledge I could. I recall that a more experienced aviator once told me that by the time I'd logged fifty traps (carrier arrested landings), I would be able to break at the bow of the ship. Breaking at the bow as opposed to a mile or two upwind is cool, mainly because it looks cool, and you're close enough to the ship so that the troops on the deck can enjoy it. Highly experienced aviators can break at the stern of the ship. Breaking early means that you have less time to slow down and configure the airplane for landing.

I took this statement to heart and began counting my shipboard landings. Forty-eight... forty-nine... At fifty, I found myself breaking the deck, i.e., the first to land on a recovery. I entered the pattern doing five hundred knots. At the bow of the ship, I pulled the throttles back to idle and started a five and a half "G" turn to downwind. I rolled out at two hundred seventy. Gear speed in the Tomcat is two-fifty, and the flaps come down at two twenty-five. So, I started my turn to final, still at idle and had only just lowered the gear. I was at the ninety when I threw the flaps down. Seconds later, still at idle, I rolled out wings level and still fast. I looked up to see the wave-off lights already flashing. I should note that all Navy Jets drop their hooks when holding above the ship prior to recovery.

Perhaps it's not intuitively obvious, but if you're fast, the airplane's angle of attack is flatter, and as a result, the hook touch down point is higher and, therefore, occurs much farther down the runway on the deck of the ship. As a result, being on speed is a requirement when landing on a ship. Otherwise, you are likely to be going around to try again.

Now the important part of the story is this: the spool-up time for the P&W TF-30 engine is sixteen seconds. It takes sixteen seconds for the motors to go from idle to military power. When a jet rolls out onto final, it's referred to as the "groove." Normal groove length is fifteen seconds. Recall that I'd been at idle for some time. Starting to recognize the problem? When the wave-off lights came on, like any trained Naval Aviator, I advanced the throttles to military power to go around. I did as I was trained, but nothing happened. Meanwhile, the airplane is slowing down. I went to max power (zone five afterburner), and still, nothing. I crossed the ramp with a centered ball on speed and caught a three-wire. On film, it looked perfect. I was rolling back in the wires, wave-off lights still flashing angrily, when the engines finally spooled up. The stark realization that, had I missed the wires, we would have gone swimming was not lost on even my pea-sized brain.

My Skipper, who was manning the Alert fifteen, had watched the whole thing up close and personal. He caught me in the passageway after the hop and said, "Sneezer, I saw your pass. Looked pretty good. Kinda quiet, though." Skipper was the king of understatement. Sadly, although stories like this are the exception, they are liberally sprinkled throughout the early years of my time as a Black Knight.

Yet, it wasn't simply my airborne performance that had me constantly skating on thin ice. One of my first jobs was as Public Affairs Officer. One of the adjunct duties of the PAO is to raise money for "squadron admins" during deployment. Squadron admins are simply the officer's suite during ports of call. Done correctly, a good PAO goes ashore with a wad of cash, secures the swankiest hotel suite money can buy, stocks the bar, fills the tub with ice and beer, and plans parties for his fellow officers while ashore. Typically, a few days ashore, done right, isn't cheap. Naval Aviators on liberty make any college fraternity look like prepubescent children in the local church bell choir.

The other part of this equation is that the Public Affairs Officer is responsible for earning money while at sea so that the squadron's admins are epic. The entrepreneurial PAO can fund a large portion of a Squadron's admins for an entire cruise. One of the ways they can do this is by selling various squadron and cruise patches while at sea. The customer base is indeed a captive audience. More importantly, it's an audience primed for the purchase of military paraphernalia, especially if it commemorates a cruise of which they are an integral part.

I'd developed a patch with garish colors and loud graphics and a caption that read, "Don't have a cow, CAG. It's only a cruise." I initially ordered five hundred. After they'd arrived, I looked for the earliest opportunity to sell them. That opportunity came only a few days later. I spent an afternoon down on the enlisted mess deck. I sold patches—four hundred and ninety-nine—that afternoon. I priced them at five dollars. I retained one patch for posterity's sake, as I was certain to go down in the annals of history as the most successful PAO ever. I was already envisioning the revenue that I'd generate with future sales.

We had an all officers meeting (AOM) that afternoon, so I shut down, deposited nearly twenty-five hundred dollars in the ship's bank, and strolled up to the AOM, to the inevitable accolades of my storied accomplishment.

I walked into the ready room and looked for my chair. I was in the same row as Mean Jim, who, at the time, was our squadron's Maintenance Officer.

"Sneezer, you sell any patches today?" he said.

"A few," I answered proudly as I handed him the last of my inventory.

Mean Jim took it. After a moment, his body began to shake, and I realized that he was laughing. Wordlessly and red-faced, he handed the patch back and waved me off as he wiped tears from his face. I assumed he just liked the patch.

I showed it to the President of the Mess, our Executive Officer. That's great, Sneeze. Let me show it to the Skipper. I'd just found my seat when the Skipper entered.

"Skipper, look at the patches Sneezer sold today," the XO said, handing him the one unsold patch that was left.

Skipper took it in his hand and looked at it for some time, a strange little smile starting to form. Finally, he looked up directly at me and asked, "You sold these?"

"Yes, sir," I answered proudly.

"How many did we sell?" he asked.

"All of them, sir," I said, still not reading the room.

"Well, can we get 'em back?"

I walked in thinking I was a hero. With those few words, I was suddenly feeling like the village idiot.

"Sneezer, you can't tell me how many?"

"About five hundred, sir."

"Well, who approved 'em?"

I glanced toward the front of the ready room and watched the XO sort of sink into his chair.

Several things rushed to the forefront of my noggin. In six months, the XO—the current President of the Officer's Mess and, as such, the person who had approved my design for the patch—would become the new skipper. My current CO stood before us, trying mightily to control his mounting anger. I looked at him rather sheepishly but remained silent.

The damage was done. Now the skipper would have to go see the Carrier Air Group Commander (his boss, the CAG) and explain why hundreds of sailors would be walking around with a patch that reminded him not to give birth to a baby bovine.

"Sneezer, I'm so mad at you right now. I don't think I can talk to you." With that, he turned on his heels and left the ready room. Junior officers sat in stunned silence as the shortest AOM (all officers meeting) anyone had ever seen ended.

I have a positive learning curve, but no one ever described it as steep. I always got better. Unfortunately, the rate at which I improved could only be described as laborious. Moreover, my general demeanor, always outwardly happy, had started to suffer. Fighter guys would rather die than look bad. Depression is a sign of weakness. Yet, I thought of all the things I was missing at home. I slept a lot. So much so that when fellow JOs met me in the passageway, their standard greeting was a loud yawn. I'd missed so much. These were pre-internet days. Skype didn't exist. Communication with hearth and home was via letter or the occasional phone call in port.

I don't know if it's something you take for granted. My dad was always there for me. He taught me how to be a good man and, more importantly, what it takes to be a good dad. So, early in my Naval career, it took a toll when I saw my oldest son's first haircut on video about a month after it had happened. And yes, VHS was all the rage. There were no uploads, no memory sticks, or no podcasts. It's worse than that, though. Earlier in the cruise, I was in a bar in Honolulu, working my way toward the bottom of my third or fourth Mai Tai, when the skipper came up to me with a serious look on his face.

"Sneezer, you need to call your wife. There's a payphone right outside the door."

Sherri had miscarried. She had to go through that horrible event all alone. Meanwhile, I was getting drunk in Hawaii.

Entitled, selfish, conceited, and narcissistic are all words describing my life back then. Yet rather than spiraling into some sort of manifesto of self-loathing, please allow me to continue.

As the cruise progressed, despite the skipper's hat-in-hand visit to the CAG to explain the "Don't Have A Cow" patch, our mess funded epic admins all over the world for that entire cruise, but it wasn't with the "Don't Have A Cow" patch. They're now a collector's item.

I'd entered the Navy supremely confident in my plan. I'd been intent on achieving fame and notoriety as an aviator, then as an entrepreneur, and perhaps finally by inspiring the masses as a successful and beloved politician. Yet despite my lackluster performance as a fighter pilot and Naval Officer, as well as mounting depression stemming from an extended absence from my young family, there was this insidious need to fly.

It's like a drug. The more you do it, the more you want to do it. More is never enough. Cheating death becomes a powerful elixir. Yes, I know that cheating death sounds like gross exaggeration, but if you've ever landed on a ship at night with a pitching deck or a wounded bird, or perhaps all of the above, you know that I'm only reporting the news.

It didn't happen all of a sudden, but at some point, the course of my life slowly changed again. Halfway through my first cruise, working for a Commanding Officer that was growing to despise me and suffering from depression—admittedly undiagnosed—I decided that I'd stop flying fighters when the job stopped being fun. That never happened.

We'd made it through the Straits of Malacca and were sailing toward our next port of call, Diego Garcia, a small island in the Indian Ocean. It was the first of August, and I was anxious for a little R&R on the beach. I was already looking forward to our next port of call, Mombasa, Kenya. I dozed off that night, dreaming of a safari.

I was awakened by the shaking of the ship as it strained mightily. I did not know where we were heading but based on the speed, wherever it was, we were in a great hurry to get there. I looked up at the Platt (the ship's TV station) and noted with surprise that we were heading north. It was August 2nd, 1990. Saddam Hussein's forces had invaded Kuwait.

Forty-eight hours later, our ship, USS Independence, became the first aircraft carrier to transit the Strait of Hormuz since the 1970s. We would spend the next three and a half months steaming around in the Persian Gulf and dreaming of the opportunity for combat.

Warriors seek war only if they are untested. Combat veterans who've been there seldom crave a second helping. That said, every pilot and Naval Flight Officer (NFO) aboard wanted to see the elephant. Ridiculous as it may sound, I'm certain that I wasn't alone in this. I prayed for war and the opportunity to test my skills in combat. As the first American Forces in the theater, we were flying missions almost continuously over Saudi Arabia in the hope that our presence would dissuade Iraqi forces from pushing further south into the Saudi oil fields.

Vigilance and readiness were constant watchwords. We spent nearly every waking moment planning for missions we would most certainly fly. Eventually. Aerial tacticians debated how airstrikes would be conducted. After about a week, other forces began to pour in. In a month or two, the Independence and its entire air wing, once the tip of the spear for all US forces in the region, was but a small cog in a gigantic multinational war machine. Schedules and mission tasking became onerous monstrosities. We flew a lot, but our piece of the ATO (Air Tasking Order) kept shrinking as USAF (Air Force) assets poured into the theatre. Still, everyone said, "Any day, any day. Be ready."

CINC CENTCOM, General Schwarzkopf, flew aboard and gave us a pep talk one steamy afternoon in the hangar bay. He told us we were all heroes because we had made Saddam hesitate. We were the first force on the scene in what was codenamed "Desert Shield." He ended by reminding us to be ready. Any day, any day. Meanwhile, the first inkling of doubt began to sneak into our psyche. Yet, no one really believed that the war we prayed for would somehow happen without us.

One evening the skipper announced that it would happen in ninety-six hours. "Get ready," he said. When it did, the operation would be called "Desert Storm." I thought back to a time long ago when I'd fought in a pitched battle somewhere over the Pacific from the friendly confines of my horse trailer. Now, it was about to get real.

Yet, in October, we started steaming east. We'd been relieved by the USS Midway, CAG Five (Carrier Air

Group), homeported in Yokosuka, Japan. Before we left the Gulf, the Battleship Missouri pulled alongside for a send-off. More importantly, the hospital ship, SS Comfort, brimming with female nurses, sent us off with a smile as they all came to the rails to wave us bon voyage.

Despite our departure, we remained certain that we were only headed to Subic Bay to get the flight deck resurfaced. After four months at sea, all the non-skid was gone, and we were landing and taxiing on bare steel. It was kind of like ice skating for airplanes. Steel coated with jet fuel and hydraulic fluid is slick. Rumor was that we were just pulling in for a quick resurface job, and then we would be heading back to the Persian Gulf for the war.

Of course, when we left the Philippines and headed east, the rumor morphed to accommodate this development. The necessary equipment and personnel were not stationed at Subic but were at Pearl.

Still, no one believed that after nearly four months in the Persian Gulf, we would not participate in the war.

Meanwhile, my piloting skills, still not eye-watering, were acceptable. My buddy Dozer had become a Landing Signal Officer (LSO). They are the people who stand out on the platform and critique and grade your landings. They occasionally actually aid when the deck is moving in heavy seas. In WWII, they were the guys that held up paddles to communicate aircraft attitude and to tell pilots when to cut power or, if necessary, wave off. LSOs don't use paddles anymore. It's all over the radio now, but to this day, their callsign on the radio is "Paddles."

In November, we picked up Tigers at Pearl Harbor for the cruise back to San Diego. "Tiger Cruise" is when the Navy invites civilians, typically family members (in those days, it was male relatives only), to embark on the final leg of the cruise back to Homeport. My dad flew out to Hawaii for the experience. Everyone was happy to see a loved one and to show them a bit of the shipboard routine.

For a time, we suspended our hawkish sentiments in favor of sharing the experience. Out of Pearl, for six days, we steamed east. On the sixth day, all the air wings flew off Indy to their respective home bases. I was the last Tomcat to fly off. My dad filmed the launch. He was on the bridge, sitting in the Captain's chair. He was conversing with the ship's CO while filming the launch from the quiet comfort of the bridge!

Back on dry land, we taxied in and shut down. Wives, girlfriends, whole families, and a host of well-wishers welcomed us back to Naval Air Station Miramar. Driving a Tomcat—or any fighter—past a gathering of enthusiastic onlookers is pretty heady stuff. I felt like a conquering hero as the engines wound down. Being a Navy fighter pilot is a series of the highest peaks and the lowest valleys.

Lowest valleys: on January 17th, 1991, while standing in our ready room in San Diego, California, I watched the first Gulf War begin. I would miss the war. Highest peaks: in February, Sherri and I found out that we were expecting our second child.

Missing the war was a bitter pill to swallow. That said, there wasn't a lot of time to sulk. In 1991, I slept in my own bed for fifty nights. A lot of things happened in those months. My flight leader, "Spud," left the squadron. I became a flight leader myself. It was announced that USS Independence would replace USS Midway as our nation's forward-deployed carrier in Yokosuka, Japan. I guess that's why we had to get back to the states. We started work-ups immediately. We'd meet later in the year in Pearl Harbor—Indy and Midway—and swap out air wings. Carrier Air Group Fourteen would go back to the United States on Midway. Carrier Air Group Five would go back to Japan aboard Independence with—for the first time—Tomcats.

I was on a four-plane detachment to Fallon, Nevada, where, for the first time in years, F-14s dropped bombs. We did workups which included an air wing detachment to Fallon, a Pineapple Cruise to Hawaii, and back. Late that summer, we moved to Japan. I did a Trans-Pacific flight with other Tomcats across the pond. We went from San Diego to Hickam,[15] Hickam to Wake Island, Wake to Guam,[16] and then Guam to Naval Air Facility, Atsugi, Japan.

In August, I rejoined Independence in Hawaii. After a couple of weeks at sea, the new CAG Five reached Subic Bay in the Philippines. Initially, there were more than a few growing pains. Integrating Tomcats with an Air Wing who'd never had them was sort of like adding oil to water. Adding us to the mix wasn't exactly an automatic thing. Tomcats were coming from a world where, right or wrong, we'd been at the top of the food chain. In actuality, Tomcats were fast approaching the end of their useful lives. Compounding the issue was the comment that we heard time and again in brief after brief, "Well, that's fine, but that's not how we did it in the war." This comment, from the "Warriors of Westpac," was like fingernails on a chalkboard for people who had spent more time in the gulf but missed the most important forty days of the entire period. Behind closed

---

[15] Hickam Air Force Base is in Honolulu, on the island of Oahu, Hawaii.

[16] Andersen Air Force Base is in Guam.

doors, Tomcat drivers wondered how such tactical minions had managed.

Chapter Thirteen: Tip of the Spear

Two-and-a-half weeks later, I walked off the brow in Yokosuka, Japan. Sherri and our son were there to meet me. Reunited, we all exchanged hugs and kisses, and I said, “Hi, honey. Show me where I live.” What a jerk. I count my blessings that I married Sherri and that we’re still together.

During my first cruise, I’d done my level best to ruin my career. As I mentioned before, our skipper had ranked me dead last among junior officers twice. An Officer’s Fitness Report determines the trajectory of one’s career. With the right turn of phrase, a superior officer can ruin it. Yet, though I was likely responsible for more than a few of his gray hairs, my first Skipper was careful in his write-ups of my performance not to say anything from which I could not eventually recover. Despite his personal distaste for me, he was always wise and fair.

Several of us had been asked to extend our sea tours so we could bring the Tomcat to Japan. Sherri and I discussed it, sort of. I pitched the idea that for our (read: my) career, we needed to go to Japan. From a career standpoint, it was a no-brainer. From a quality of life standpoint, domestic bliss was unlikely.

Sherri walked around the base, six months pregnant, dragging a two-year-old toddler in the August heat and humidity of the southern Kanto Plain. After a few days, she found our car and our house, then moved us in, and then after all that was done, I arrived and said, "Hi honey, show me where I live."

The operational tempo for the forward-deployed air wing is, comparatively speaking, incomparable. Other air wings may think they're busy, and I suppose they may be, but during my year in Japan, I believe I was "feet dry"[17] for a total of three months.

I was there in October. That's when our youngest son was born. We drove down to the hospital at Naval Station Yokosuka on October ninth as a mild typhoon struck. It was a good thing as the traffic was light by Japanese standards. The seventeen-mile commute only took an hour and ten minutes.

Our youngest son was born on October 10th, 1991, via Cesarean section. Sherri was initially fine, but a week later, as I left for the Philippines, she developed an infection in her incision.

Going up and down stairs in a Japanese home is sort of like an extreme sport when healthy. They're steep. If you have an infected incision, it becomes an insurmountable obstacle. Sherri moved into base housing, living with T for several weeks. Dozer and T had been our friends since our dogs met at the kennels at Naval Air Station Miramar. T got base housing when we moved to Japan because she only required a one-

---

[17] "Feet dry" means onshore and is the radio call to signify that an airplane is over land (typically inbound to the designated target). Conversely, "feet wet," is called crossing the beach outbound.

bedroom bungalow. All the larger houses were full. That is why we lived out in the community.

Japanese construction is much different than what is considered standard here in America. Central heating is a rarity. Additionally, walls tend to be paper-thin. Seriously, traditional homes were often constructed with paper walls. Though that is no longer the standard, walls have a thickness of one to two inches. The result is that on cold mornings it's not unusual to see your breath when you wake up. I've often heard the advice of keeping your shampoo in the refrigerator, so it won't freeze at night. Socks on the toilet seat were a must. In a technologically advanced society like Japan, there were countless devices for staying warm, save one, which was central heat. We heated our home with a small portable kerosene heater.

After our second son was born, I spent a week at home, and then we sailed down to the P.I. We were underway or on detachment in the Philippines for the next six to eight weeks. While we sharpened our warfighting skills as an air wing, we also enjoyed leisure time in the tropical paradise around Subic Bay. For instance, the golf course on Naval Air Station Cubi Point was unimaginably gorgeous. We did not know it then, but we were enjoying the final days in the last bastion of American Colonialism. When you pulled into Subic, you could get your shoes shined, a shave and a haircut, your laundry done, and a massage while you waited, sipping on a Cubi-Special.[18] The whole experience would cost you about five dollars American and, if you were not a stickler when it came to improbity, an extra five could buy you a lot more.

---

[18] Cubi-Special is a tropical rum infused drink concocted by Navy Pilots returning to Subic, specifically the Cubi Point Officer's club for R&R after combat duties on Yankee Station in Vietnam (recipe available online)

My longest stint on dry land that year happened upon my return to Japan. The Japanese were not happy to listen to us bounce (land-based simulated carrier landing practice) and, in the spirit of conciliation—at least so far as noise abatement was concerned—most of our landing practice happened six-hundred miles south on a tiny island in the Pacific called Iwo Jima. Yeah, that one. You can still tour many underground bunkers where Japanese Soldiers lived and fought during the ferocious WWII battle.

During those months, we were there only twice. Each trip lasted less than a week. The reason is that to remain certified to land on an aircraft carrier, pilots need at least one nighttime landing per week. If that doesn't happen, pilots must recertify (i.e., get carrier qualified again). During our time in Japan, the Ops Tempo was such that we were seldom out of Qual.

I spent the next six months—November through April—in or around Japan. Independence sortied out of Yokosuka a few times. For instance, we were part of annual exercises on the Korean Peninsula. We steamed down into the South China Sea a few times. In January, the Navy flew wives and families down to Hong Kong for a few days when we were in port there. My oldest son celebrated his third birthday there.

In March, USS Independence sortied down to the Philippines for our final tune-up prior to cruise. We had an epic party at the NAS Cubi Point O-Club. "The Final Fling," hosted by the two Tomcat squadrons, commemorated the last visit of a US Navy carrier battle group prior to the Subic Bay naval complex being turned back over to the Philippine government.

My friend Slim designed and then oversaw the construction of this huge ramp shaped like an aircraft carrier. People rode down tracks that were sky blue in a simulated airplane and could drop a hook to catch a wire and thus stop. If successful, the ship's island housed this dunk tank, and senior officers took turns getting dunked. If the person riding down the rails missed the wires, he went off the end into a pool. It was quite something and became a most popular pastime. It was an epic party, and though no one probably remembers all of it, everyone had a good time, and we started to assimilate into our newly-reconstituted air wing. Later that evening, I believe Slim may have invented the "Selfie" as we attempted to capture ourselves projectile vomiting off of the second-floor balcony at the Cubi Point BOQ.[19] Our attempts were unsuccessful. Bored, we checked on a group from our air wing in a room nearby.

We stepped in to pay our respects and converse with our new air wing mates from one of the Hornet squadrons. We had been talking for several minutes when it dawned on us that we were the only people in the room wearing a stitch of clothing. There were four naked aviators and five naked women, pros flown in from Manila. Slim and I, having sobered up a bit, realized what we had stumbled into and beat a hasty retreat.

Whether it was strippers in Hong Kong or prostitutes in the P.I., or benny boys in Singapore, unlike Icarus, I was constantly on the outskirts of not the sun but utter darkness. "Join the Navy, see the world" should have been "Join the Navy, see human depravity on an industrial scale."

A junior officer told a story about going home with a local barfly one night in Olongapo (The Philippines). Just before hopping into the sack, she asked politely,

---

[19] Bachelor's Officer's Quarters

"Would you mind if I remove my leg?" Sure enough, she removed her prosthetic device and hung it on the wall. In the morning, shafts of sunshine poured through the shack's slatted walls, and a rooster perched on his chest crowed right in his face! GOOD MORNING! WAKEY, WAKEY!

Back then, my initial reaction was laughter at this funny little story. Yet the abject poverty of the one-legged prostitute, born into a world of squalor, was not even given a moment's consideration. That is because, at that point in my life, everything revolved around my will, not God's. I had nearly a decade of living yet to do before this revelation would solidify. "There is a big difference between free will and God's will."[20]

As we embarked on our cruise in April of 1992, my second, I had mixed feelings. I left on the day my youngest son took his first bite of solid food. The next time I saw him, he was starting to talk. Yet, on the other hand, flying was my passion. My life had taken another, albeit insidious, turn. I no longer cared about politics or history or wealth or cementing my name on the pathway of history. I just wanted to fly, preferably in combat, and to get as good at it as my God-given abilities would allow. I would stop flying jets when I stopped having fun.

In retrospect, this was simply me substituting one gargantuan dose of narcissism for another. Flying a jet fighter is the ultimate adrenaline rush. I suspect it's akin to drug addiction. The more you do it, the more you want to do it. The sheer joy is, of course, transitory. The point being is that it forces all other important things in one's life to become secondary. It is selfishness beyond belief. It's a kick in the pants, though. I've heard it described as the most fun you can have with your

---

[20] Mirjana Soldo, "My Heart Will Triumph," pg. 183

clothes on. That's one of the most succinct descriptions I've heard.

We were soon in the Persian Gulf once again, and this time "Green Ink"[21] was common. In July of 1992, President George H. W. Bush announced a "no-fly zone" over Iraq. The United States, United Kingdom, and France would protect the Kurds in northern Iraq and Shiites in the south by limiting Iraqi air operations to an area between the 32nd and 36th parallels of latitude. Iraqi aircraft south of thirty-two degrees or north of thirty-six were considered hostile.

Yet a lot happened before the no-fly zone was announced. Early in my career, someone told me if you were readily available to fly and made it known to the people in operations that a fleet Naval Aviator could expect one-thousand hours in type and three hundred traps by the time they reached the end of their sea tour. I took this to heart, and by the time I left, I wanted to be wearing a thousand-hour patch and at least three one-hundred trap patches. Consequently, I let it be known that I would happily take all the traps I could get day or night. Silly me. This meant that I would be a fixture on the night page.

My first RIO was Tiger. He taught me nearly everything I know about fighter aviation. When I was a nugget (new guy), our flight lead was Spud, and what Tiger didn't teach me, Spud did. Spud's RIO was another nugget, callsign Lulu.

---

[21] In a Navy pilot's logbook, black ink is used to record daytime operations, red ink is used to record nighttime, and green ink denotes combat.

On my second cruise, I was now a flight lead, and Lulu was my RIO. It didn't take long for me to appreciate Lulu as a person and as a RIO, and still, I managed to underestimate him. Lulu possessed intellectual agility that could have bred disdain and intolerance for the less quick-witted mortals surrounding him—i.e., pretty much everyone, especially me—but that was never the case. Despite being the smartest person in the room—almost always—a level of deference existed. Lulu was willing to subvert his powerful intellect to allow others around him to shine. I myself did not fully comprehend this chameleon-like ability until years later.

Now, on account of my big mouth, Lulu and I were flying at night a lot. Besides being a great RIO, Lulu took no small measure of pride in concocting and then telling funny little stories for the pilots with whom he flew. While we "bored holes in the sky" in the "marshall stack,"[22] he would regale us with these intricate and pointless tales to take our minds off the impending terror we were about to experience. I heard all his stories, and in retrospect, I suppose "The Grape Ape" or "Sam the Clam's Disco" was not so pointless after all. Pushing out of the stack for a night trap is not for the faint of heart. A few minutes of distraction provided by a master storyteller was a most therapeutic remedy.

I lived in a three-man stateroom forward on the O2 level. The room was about six by nine. I'm always reminded of Sir Winston Churchill's quote that "serving aboard a ship is a lot like a prison with a slightly increased risk of drowning." That small area filled with

---

[22] Nighttime holding pattern where jets are stacked up for eventual recovery

F-14 aircrew was commonly referred to as "Sleepy Hollow." Down on the O2 level, and forward as it was, the constant banging of airplanes landing on the roof or of catapult launches were not heard. I lived there with two other pilots in my squadron, Sweat and Tag. Halfway through the cruise, Tag's sea tour ended, and my RIO, Lulu, moved in. One might suspect that living and flying together could eventually cause some angst but, speaking solely for myself, we never had a cross word or malevolent thought. The spice was always provided by Sweat. A professional pot-stirrer if ever there was one. I smile every time I think about him.

An ornery SOB, Sweat is a high PRF[23] guy. Originally from Jersey, he thinks fast, talks faster, and he's funny. It was indeed a privilege to live with those guys. Sometimes I would just sit back and listen to them.

In late summer, Lulu got paired with Montana. They were Skipper's pick for Top Gun. I got to fly with a new batch of RIOs. No longer a nugget but now an experienced fleet Naval Aviator, I was getting paired with all the first-cruise RIOs.

It was not more than two weeks after Monty and Lulu shipped off for San Diego (the Naval Fighter Weapons School, Top Gun, was at NAS Miramar in San Diego, California) that we started "no-fly zone" operations. These were typically seven-hour missions. Getting gas airborne was now old hat. As mentioned, these were classified as combat missions. While some senior F-14 guys were attempting to get enough

---

[23] PRF – Pulse Repetition Frequency (PRF) is the number of pulses of a repeating signal in a specific time unit, normally measured in pulses per second. The term is used within a number of technical disciplines, notably radar. Higher PRF requires a more powerful radar and thus more energy. Consequently, a high PRF person has a lot of energy.

missions to qualify for air medals, I found it somewhat distasteful to call what we did combat. We had a hard deck that was high enough that only SAMs[24] would be able to shoot at us. To my knowledge, I don't believe I was ever shot at. Nor did I ever fire a shot in anger. We came close, though.

One day members of the Iraqi Air Force were flying south at tactical airspeeds right up to the 32nd parallel, and then they would break left or right to avoid becoming a fireball. I suppose they were taunting us. Perhaps they were trying to create some sort of international incident? We were armed with Phoenix missiles that day and could have easily made it rain small pieces of MIG, but our rules of engagement stated that we were only authorized to fire if aircraft were south of latitude thirty-two. We were hoping, praying really, that they would accidentally get too far south. They never did.

My last trap in a Tomcat occurred at three o'clock in the morning in September of Nineteen ninety-two. In my final month as an F-14 pilot, I suddenly found my mojo as a driver. I'd become a capable warrior and the airplane, for one brief shining moment, felt like an extension of my body. I'd end just shy of one-thousand hours but did surpass three-hundred carrier landings. That morning was my one hundred tenth night landing.

I had finally broken the code and tamed the Tomcat. I was most certainly full of myself as I came down the pike. On final, the ball was centered, and that's where it stayed. I was certain my last trap in the F-14 was an "Okay" pass.

---

24 Surface to Air Missile

Yet, the chasm between perception and reality is sometimes a great yawning abyss. I was back on the throttles crossing the ramp and caught the three-wire. I went to military upon touchdown, then quickly back to idle as I felt the tug and the airplane's sudden deceleration. Consequently, the landing signal officers assumed—incorrectly—that I'd landed at idle.

I climbed out of the jet and made my way below to maintenance and the ready room. At this point, I'm all happy.

I walked into one door in maintenance as Dozer entered from the opposite door and the ready room.

"Sneezer, how's it going?"

"Hey, Dozer. Okay Three, right?"

"Snee, if I wasn't on the platform just now, they would've given you a Cut Pass."

"A CUT? You gotta be shittin' me!" I said, instantly hot. "I crossed the ramp, went to mil,[25] felt the tug, and went back to idle. I had a centered ball all the way. Dozer, that was one of the best passes I ever flew."

"Whisper Jet. It's dark. They can't see the cans. All they can do is go by the sound. I talked 'em down to a no grade, though."

"So, be happy with my no grade?"

"It sucks, but it's not like it's gonna be your last trap ever."

---

[25] Military Power is simply throttles full forward, i.e., maximum, but not past the throttle detent, i.e., afterburner not selected.

Chapter Fourteen: Bogey Driver

Dozer and I flew out on the last COD back to Bahrain. By then, Indy was in the Gulf of Oman[26], steaming south to eventually get back to Japan. From that point on, the CODs[27] would be coming from DGAR (Diego Garcia). Dozer and I had checked into the Black Knights on the same day. In training, we CQed together twice. Our wives were best of friends. Sherri had lived with T for a time after the birth of our youngest. Now we had departed CV-62[28] together. We were beginning the longest day of our lives. Twenty-four hours later, I shook

---

26 The Gulf of Oman (GOO) is in the Indian Ocean, well south of the Persian Gulf; not to be confused with GOO which can also mean bad weather (IFR conditions).

27 COD Carrier Onboard Delivery is a C-2 turboprop airplane that delivers small parts, passengers and most importantly the mail to a Carrier at sea.

28 CV-62 was the NATO designator for USS Independence, one of the last conventionally powered aircraft carriers. At the time it had the lowest hook to ramp clearance of any carrier in the US arsenal, including CV-43, Midway; the ship that CAG-5 had been on previously.

Dozer's hand in Philadelphia.[29] A fitting place to take our leave of one another. Three hours after that, I touched down in Des Moines, Iowa.

Sherri and our two sons, as well as her parents, picked me up at the airport. It took a couple of days for my youngest son to warm up to me. He wondered who that strange man was that kept kissing his mother.

Sherri had moved home just a month or two after we had left on cruise. I would spend most of September on leave in Iowa at the home of her parents.

In the Navy, at least with Aviators, one typically rotates between sea and shore tours. After three years and two months in VF- 154,[30] I had decided that I wanted to be an adversary pilot. One's selection is based upon one's performance. Yet, there are also subjective criteria that may enter the equation. Recall at the beginning of my time as a Black Knight, I'd been rated last among my peers. Yet when Dozer and I willingly extended to do time in Japan, coupled with my steady improvement as both an Officer and Aviator, I believe that my preferences were given more serious consideration. As such, I was granted my second choice. VFA-127[31] (Strike Fighter Squadron One Two Seven), the "Desert Bogeys," was one of two Pacific Fleet Adversary squadrons.

When it came time for me to select what I wanted to do on my shore tour, adversary pilot was it. There were four choices, VF-126 in San Diego, VF-45 in Key West, VF-43 in Oceana, and VFA-127 in Fallon, NV. I did not think I had a shot in San Diego, and moreover,

---

29 Philadelphia, Pennsylvania is the city of brotherly love.

30 Fighter Squadron 154; the Black Knights, flew the F-14 Tomcat off CV-62, USS Independence out of Naval Station Yokosuka, Japan. Ashore they were based at Naval Air Facility Atsugi, Japan.

31 VFA-127 Desert Bogeys were stationed at Naval Air Station Fallon, Nevada.

I'd made the decision that I wanted to transition from the F-14 Tomcat to the F/A-18 Hornet. I figured my chances would be better in a Strike Fighter designated squadron.

That said, I do love Key West. So, I put both choices down. My thinking was if I got Key West, we'd buy a boat and lots of fishing tackle, maybe even some scuba gear. I had first learned to dive in Guam. Dozer taught me. If it were Fallon, I'd get a four-wheel drive and some hunting and camping gear. In other words, I was ready to embrace both worlds. I ended up driving an old Toyota 4-Runner.

We left Iowa in late September and headed west. Fallon is about two hours east of Reno, NV. In WWII, it had been part of a string of airbases intended to quell a Japanese invasion that never came. Later it became the US Navy's primary over-land training facility. Today, as the home of both the Naval Strike Air Warfare Center (NSAWC) and the Naval Fighter Weapons School (Top Gun), it still is.

For fighter pilots, it is heaven. Adversary pilots fly ACM (air combat maneuvering) hops all day long. Then at night, they go home to mom and the kids. To call it idyllic is not an overstatement. Training to be an Adversary Instructor Pilot is rigorous. Eventually, you get good. I felt as though I had a small advantage. In the Tomcat, I was a fighter pilot. Our mission was singular and focused. I had the unparalleled advantage of having flown with world-class experts like Tiger and Spud and a mafia of folks who had been or soon would be Top Gun instructors. In contrast, many VFA-127 adversary pilots had, by definition, come from the Attack and later Fighter/Attack communities. Naval Aviators from any community are consummate pros, but—and perhaps this is based solely upon my own bias—Tomcat drivers walked in the door with a huge advantage.

My many good friends from the fighter/attack community will likely disagree, and, for most of my fellow bogey drivers, I gracefully concede. VFA-127's syllabus brought everyone who strapped on a jet to a virtuoso level of performance very quickly. Any perceived advantage that I may have had initially quickly vanished, and in the long run, I was, as is my modus operandi, average.

Yet, I was average among a cadre of the finest Aviators I've ever known. I soon found myself as a newly-minted Adversary Instructor Pilot. I'd been there about a year when I, too, attended Top Gun, then still in San Diego. This was great because I brought Sherri and the boys with me. Dozer and T were in the Fleet Replacement Squadron (FRS) down there in VF-124, the place where we'd first met. As a seasoned Landing Signal Officer (LSO), Dozer was a valuable commodity in the FRS.

As we drove south past the Joshua trees, we were entering a magical period, indeed the "salad days" of our lives. "For a moment, all the world was right."[32]

The Navy Fighter Weapons school effectively has two tracks. In the first, Fleet Aviators are chosen by their respective squadron COs. The second track is composed of Adversary pilots, who are the bandits (red forces) that simulate enemy tactics. Everyone goes through the academic portion (i.e., ground school) together. Then for the next couple of weeks, Top Gun Instructors lead the Red Force (enemy) in elaborate simulated multi-ship DACM (Dissimilar Air Combat Maneuvering) scenarios that are conducted to train both

---

32 "The Dance," by Tony Arata, performed by Garth Brooks

fleet aviators and bandits. At least, that is how it used to be. I'm told that today the red forces (adversary forces) are all outsourced to reservists or civilian organizations.

At any rate, upon our return to the high desert, I was soon leading four ships on DACM missions against invading blue forces. I was coaching my oldest son in soccer and baseball. Sherri had many great friends and neighbors, Chatty Kathy, Dr. Ebay, Angie, Ann, Terri, Susan, Luce, and Connie, to name a few.

We hung around with other bogeys and their families, great friends. I hunted Muley's with Pops, Donk, Alien, Tonka, and our skipper, Wild Hair. I chased elk and hunted mule deer with my friend Chaplain White (then the Lutheran Minister at NAS Fallon). We hunted wild hogs with Alien and one of his Stanford buds in the foothills above San Jose. Montana, who had been a Black Knight with me in the fleet, joined us for many of those excursions, as did our buddy Toes. For a guy from Iowa, hunting and fishing out west was an adventure.

In those days, we typically flew twice a day. Every so often, bogey drivers flew three times. Rarely one might fly just one time. It was an extreme anomaly not to find your name on the schedule at least one time. Our hops were normally against the F/A-18 Hornet FRS (fleet replacement squadron students). VFA-125, out of NAS Lemoore, California, had baked an entire DACM syllabus into their training regimen. To satisfy this requirement, detachments of perspective Hornet drivers would come to Fallon to fight us. The training syllabus progressed from 1v1s against F-5s to unknown numbers of dissimilar aircraft simulating the tactics of potential threats. We also flew hops against fleet squadrons in a training program known as FFARP (Fleet Fighter Air Combat Maneuvering Readiness Program) and against entire air wings cycling through their more advanced training at the Naval Strike and Air Warfare Center.

During slack times, which were few, we managed to hone our skills fighting the USAF from Mountain Home[33] or Hill AFB.[34] Additionally, we would participate in Red Flag[35] at Nellis down near Las Vegas. Finally, the most fun would be our annual pilgrimage to FWIC (Fighter Weapons Instructor Course—Canada's Top Gun) in Cold Lake, Canada. Here the days were spent flying and fighting the Canucks. Nighttime is where a guy could get into trouble.

Whether we were racing rental cars at one hundred-ten mph up a gravel road to the lake to fish or frequenting the local watering holes—all replete with strippers—or taking a field trip to Edmonton, fighter guys are typically looking for trouble. Usually, they find it.

My little sister was married during one of my trips to Cold Lake. Of course, like many of the important events in my family, I missed it.

During my last trip to Cold Lake, I was the OIC (Officer in Charge) of our detachment. On a field trip to Edmonton, after a thousand-dollar bar tab and too many White Russians, I did my best Elvis karaoke and later swam in the Lagoon at the Edmonton Mall. Good times. I am told.

---

[33] Air Force base near Boise, Idaho.

[34] Air Force base near Salt Lake City, Utah.

[35] Red Flag is the U.S. Air Force's premier air-to-air combat training exercise. Participants often include both the United States and allied nations' combat air forces. The exercise provides aircrews the experience of multiple, intensive air combat sorties in the safety of a training environment.

Here's the deal, during the first year and a half of a tour with the Desert Bogeys, I'd managed to become a well-respected adversary pilot, and when it came time for our Skipper to choose a new Assistant Operations Officer—one of the more esteemed positions for JOs (Junior Officers), he picked me. The decision tree that happened was well above my pay grade, but I suspect that the previous assistant ops O—my good friend, Pops—may have put in a favorable word for me. The other highly likely scenario is that as the most senior JO in the squadron, it made sense that I had been given the opportunity. I was the most senior JO because I had been med-down for several months early in my Naval career.

When I was a Black Knight, I had been ranked dead last among other JOs early in my tour. Now I would finish the last half of my tour as a Desert Bogey consistently ranked number one. That remarkable turn of fate reminds me of a Glen Campbell song, "Rhinestone Cowboy," 'there's been a load of comprimisin' on the road to my horizon.' See, a monkey could have run operations in VFA-127. Case in point, me.

Bogey drivers are not selected from the bottom of the heap. They tend to have been top performers in their respective fleet squadrons. As a result, they never had to be told where to be or what to do. Truth be told, it was highly likely that, were we all in a fleet squadron together, I would have been the lowest ranking individual among them.

There were five other junior officers who took turns writing the daily schedule. All were significantly more intelligent than me. Additionally, there was an absence of tension between Operations and Maintenance. Ops writes a schedule based upon the number of sorties it needs with respect to the operations tempo. In turn, maintenance will give them what they can. In VFA-127, we had civilian-staffed contract maintenance. That contract incorporated a penalty schedule, i.e., contractors were penalized if they could not produce enough "up" airplanes to meet the daily schedule. It was rare that we could not generate the required number of sorties due to some maintenance limitation. Thus, my relatively simple task was scheduling our operations on a macro-level while tracking the budget. On a squadron level, my main job was to fly. Operations and the entire squadron ran like the well-oiled machine that it was. All I really did was stand back and watch.

Talk about a dream job. I often rode my bike to work since we were less than a mile from the front gate in base housing. I flew F-5s and F/A-18s by day. I raced go-carts with other pilots at the local track on base, camped, fly-fished, and hunted in the fall. I coached both of my sons in little league. At night I would eat supper with my family. At bedtime, I slept with my wife. Being the AOPSO (Assistant Operations Officer) of a bogey squadron is the best job there is.

As I climbed the stairs to the top deck of hangar four each morning, I took the stairs two at a time, singing. I played it cool as I entered the ready room, but it was difficult because I loved my job so much. I have so many great friends scattered all about the country, all of whom were once steely-eyed killers who trained countless other Navy Fighter guys to be steely-eyed killers too. I mentioned earlier that once upon a time, the best fighter pilots lived in San Diego and flew great big airplanes. While that may have been true then, in a little "cow town" in the high desert, I got to fly with the best there ever was. I was Joe Average, but I was Joe Average among the finest assemblage of fighter pilots I have ever known.

I wanted, as Maslow might have said, to achieve self-actualization as a fighter pilot. I believe, at least in the visual arena, that I did. I was as good as I would have ever gotten. I could fight the jet on the edge of the envelope, take notes about the fight as it was happening, instruct the student across the circle, give him pointers and encouragement in real-time over the radio, give him a chance to win in his vastly superior airplane and if he could not get it done, kill him. Then lead him back to the field where, in the debrief, I would take an hour or two, pointing out how things could have gone better. The real teachable moments are on the ground well after the fight.

What I have just described is what all average Bogey Drivers did daily. That said, an average Bogey Driver is not average.

In my time as a Bogey Driver, as in the fleet, I would experience a few close calls, an engine failure here, a close pass there. Listing them all would be tedious for me and boring for you. Naval Aviation is still a dangerous business. Yet surviving unscathed was always chalked up to the "it's better to be lucky than good" dictum. Now that I am older, perhaps wiser, I believe there was more to it than luck.

In the fall of Nineteen ninety-five, after only three attempts, I drew a Desert Bighorn sheep tag. Locals who had been dutifully entering the lottery for decades suddenly turned icy. My good friend "Alien" had drawn a tag two years earlier and offered to guide me.

I'd first met Alien on a dive in the Persian Gulf. He was in CAG[36] Five in VFA-192,[37] the World Famous Golden Dragons, one of the two Hornet Squadrons aboard Indy. We had both surfaced at roughly the same moment and were hanging onto the gunnels of the small dingy we had ridden out to the dive site when I casually introduced myself by opening my mouth and promptly inserting my foot.

"Hi, I'm Sneezer."

"Alien."

"You're a Chippy[38], right?" The Chippies were the other Hornet squadron in the air wing.

"No, I'm a Dragon."

"Oh," I said dumbly as he swam away.

Now, nearly three years later, "Alien" and I were bogey drivers. We often flew together. Our families were close.

About a week into my sheep hunt, we spotted a small bachelor herd across a valley well above us. For the next several hours, we climbed around the backside of the mountain to work ourselves into a position for a shot. The more we climbed, the slower I went. As we neared the top, the going became somewhat treacherous. The path, if one could call it such, was littered with loose shale and strewn with not-so-small boulders. The backside of this hill was steeper than the side where we had last spotted the sheep. Near the crest, we had to leap from rock to rock across

---

[36] CAG or Carrier Air Group is the air wing attached to a particular aircraft carrier. Sometimes the acronym is CVW; which stands for Carrier Air Wing as CV is the NATO abbreviation for an aircraft carrier. CVN is a Nuclear Carrier.

[37] Japan based Strike Fighter Squadron One Ninety-Two, VFA-192 the "Golden Dragons," radio callsign "Dragon."

[38] Japan based Strike Fighter Squadron One Ninety-Five, VFA-195 the "Dam Busters," radio callsign "Chippy."

precipitous voids. One misstep might send you plummeting a thousand feet to the sage-covered valley below. I leaped to a boulder where Alien stood waiting. I was wearing a mostly empty backpack, and the small amount of weight left me somewhat top-heavy. When I landed, my higher center of gravity would have toppled me off the rock and sent me plummeting toward oblivion, save the fact that Alien casually reached out to steady me.

I know Alien probably does not recall the event, but it is certain that had he not been there, my children would have grown up without a father. Additionally, knowing what I now know, I wonder if this seemingly innocuous loss of balance was not a precursor to my future.

I could have spent the rest of this book regaling you with stories from my time in the Navy. There are so many things I have not shared. Flying was my passion. Being an adversary pilot was the best job I've ever had. Best job anyone has ever had, if you can call it a job, and keep a straight face. I had the privilege of associating with a passel of great people. By the way, minutes after nearly taking a swan dive into the great beyond, I did bag a Desert Bighorn.

Chapter Fifteen: Limbo

A week after my sheep hunt, my orders to the FRS at NAS Lemoore came through. I would be transitioning to the F/A-18 Hornet for my next sea tour. But not before extending once again until VFA-127 shut down. No one was happy about it, but all active duty Navy Adversary squadrons were being closed, and the mission was going to be handled by reservists.

Three weeks later, a bunch of us were gathering for Thanksgiving. I'd been running quite a bit, but a week after I'd returned from hunting sheep, I was experiencing slight numbness down my right leg. The flight surgeon had diagnosed it as sciatica and suggested that I refrain from running, lifting weights, and flying. I had told him I'd gladly comply on the first two but not flying was not an option; not only were we busy, but telling a fighter pilot he cannot fly is like telling a heroin addict that opiates should be avoided.

However, on Thanksgiving morning, there was no numbness. I'd been feeling good for about a week. So, on that morning, knowing full well that I'd spend much of the afternoon stuffing my face, I decided a run was in order. I did four miles, and although I had not run in about a month, I was pleased with my time.

By the time I'd gotten back to my front door, I could tell something wasn't quite right. I was feeling the same numbness I'd felt in my leg, except I was feeling it on the entire right side of my body. From the top of my head to the tip of my right toes, it felt as though my muscles were just waking up from a long winter's nap. Coordination, strength, everything seemed fine. Moreover, there was no pain. It just felt weird. A closer examination revealed that, indeed, it was exactly the right half of my body. At the risk of sharing too much information, in the shower, I determined that the right side of my penis felt sort of numb while the left side was normal.

It was Thanksgiving Day, and I thought it best to keep quiet and not ruin the holiday for something so trivial. Yet as the day progressed, there was no improvement. As mentioned, there was no pain, and I wondered if the run had exacerbated my sciatica once again.

Although the numbness persisted, I didn't believe it would affect my ability to fly. Additionally, like many Naval Aviators, a certain level of distrust existed between any self-respecting aviator and medicine. After all, it was the doctor's job to ground us. Recall that my Naval Career had almost ended before it began because of Doctors at NAMI.[39] Plus, we were busy. I really did not have time to go over and see a flight surgeon. So, I did not.

[39] NAMI is the Naval Aerospace Medical Institute.

Days later, I was scheduled for a two vs. two F-5's against F/A-18 Hornets from the FRS.[40] That morning's hop had me flying our only two-seat airplane. My passenger that day was our squadron's flight surgeon.

As recounted in my novella-sized memoir, *The Gift*, that morning's hop went fine. Air combat maneuvering (ACM) is a wild ride. The debrief—if I do say so myself—was also an impressive learning experience for our students.

After the hop, we wandered back into the ready room to take a moment around the "water-cooler" between flights. In casual conversation, I mentioned to the flight doc—who was reading the paper and having a cup of java before returning to the clinic—that I was again suffering from sciatica, but this time it was the entire right side of my body.

"Why don't you swing by the clinic later this afternoon, and we'll check it out?"

Still oblivious, I retorted, "I'd like to, doc, but I've got another hop this afternoon."

"No, you don't."

Three little words. And with them, my life was forever changed. The 2v2 that I had flown that morning was the last ACM hop of my life.

Less than twenty-four hours later, I had my first MRI. After the procedure, the Tech handed me some paperwork and said, "Good luck, buddy."

That afternoon the Flight Surgeon I'd flown with told me that the MRI indicated Multiple Sclerosis (MS). It was less than a month from Christmas in 1995. Initially, the prescribed treatment was a mega-dose of steroids.

---

[40] FRS is the Fleet Replacement Squadron.

In my previous attempt to document this journey, *The Gift*, I spent a page or two detailing the effects of Prednisone on the body. From five to sixty milligrams, humans tolerate Prednisone well. Yet, in higher dosages, the effects are pronounced in both the short-term and the long-term.

Prednisone is a steroid intended to limit and reduce swelling. Swelling is an issue with MS because it impedes the normal signal transmission of electrical messages traveling along the superhighway of one's nervous system. The thinking is less swelling and less permanent damage. In gargantuan doses—I was essentially getting infusions of the stuff intravenously—it is a double-edged sword. Sure, the swelling, if there was any, did go down, but Prednisone has nasty side effects. Most are short-term. More on that later.

Meanwhile, Naval Medicine began a two-year process of attempting to rule out other possibilities. Note: at this juncture, I believe I would have donated a kidney if it meant that I could fly jets again. Moreover, at this stage of my career, I was quite likely a ten-million-dollar man. The Navy had bled money to get me to this stage. My level of expertise, though average among fellow bogey drivers, was easily leaps and bounds beyond that of an average Naval Aviator. Really good fighter pilots do not grow on trees. To that end, instead of throwing me over the side as they had nearly done early in my career, the doctors scrambled to call the demyelination that had occurred in my noggin something, anything else.

After almost a year, they eventually called it Optic Neuritis, disregarding the fact that I had originally presented with numbness that was first diagnosed as sciatica. Yet, I am getting ahead of myself.

We flew home to Iowa for Christmas. Hard, even for a lukewarm Christian, to find the season depressing, but I told our family that I had experienced a neurological event and that the initial diagnosis was MS.

After returning to the high desert, my skipper got me a job at the Naval Strike and Air Warfare Center (NSAWC) across the street. The plan was that I would stay on at VFA-127 until it closed and then work as an aid to help VFC-13 settle in at Fallon. Then, while Medical attempted to get me flying again, I would work at NSAWC in a position called Fleet Liaison Officer.

Prior to our squadron's decommissioning, my skipper selected me to represent VFA-127, nominating me for Junior Officer of the year. It is called the Admiral Wesley McDonald award and is given annually to the outstanding Pacific Fleet Junior Aviator from the strike-fighter community. While simply being nominated is indeed an honor, several things come to mind. First, an adversary pilot would typically never be selected to receive this award. It is most often reserved for those in the Fleet, you know, the folks out on the "tip of the spear" who are actually "haze gray and underway." Adversaries, though technically eligible, do not win such awards because their recompense has already been received (they already have the coolest job on the planet).

The other somewhat ironic part of this whole story is that I was only technically part of the Strike Fighter community. On paper, I was an F/A-18 pilot, having received written orders stating such. Yet, in the fleet, I had been a Tomcat guy (VF, not VFA). Moreover, early on, I had been ranked dead last among my peers.

"Skipper, given my current medical issues, are you sure you want to waste this on me?" I asked one day in the ready room.

To his credit, "Moose" answered simply that "you're my choice."

"Stitch" won that year. He was not at the ceremony held at some swanky hotel in Fresno near the Navy's west coast master jet base, NAS Lemoore, CA. Stitch was at sea. I would not meet him for several more months.

After the decommissioning of the Desert Bogeys (VFA-127), I did a short stint at VFC-13 (the reserve adversary squadron replacing us). I checked in across the street at NSAWC. In those days, there were lots of moving parts in Naval Aviation. Active duty adversaries had gone away, replaced by reservists. The Navy Fighter Weapons School (Top Gun) had moved to Fallon from Miramar, which became a Marine Corps Air Station. F-14 Tomcats were moved to the East Coast, flying out of NAS Oceana when ashore. Most notably, in what can only be described as marketing genius, Top Gun was absorbed into NSAWC. Talk about killing the golden goose. Fortunately, the goose would not die. I am happy to report that today the Navy Fighter Weapons School is as vibrant as it ever was.

In my little world, to describe life as unsettled would be a gross understatement. I was no longer flying. Originally flying, now an obsession, was simply a part of the "me" I had hoped to build. I had so many other things I wanted to do. I wanted to be somebody. I planned to be someone you would remember in business or politics, or perhaps as a writer. Naval Officer, i.e., Aviator, was simply one notch in that belt. The problem is that when you start with the vocation that you are most passionate about, it is nearly impossible to stop. I would become content with the status quo. Flying fast movers was ultimately the pinnacle of my professional life. Or so I thought. I was thirty-three.

Now I was the Fleet Liaison Officer—whatever the hell that meant—at the Naval Strike and Air Strike Warfare Center (NSAWC). My responsibilities were not well-defined. It was a job created so I would have a place to hide while Medical tried to figure out my issues. I underwent a series of tests, and they occurred all up and down the west coast. There were spinal taps and batteries of neurological exams. Nothing proved conclusive.

Our boys—then seven and four—were, in my opinion, too young to understand the potential ramifications of major neurological dysfunction in their father. At this juncture, there was not much to notice. They may have recognized some decrease in the level of our physical play. That said, I could still run and pretty much do all the things I had always done with them.

When my oldest son turned three, he was gaining coordination and developing a skill set that indicated that he would someday be an athlete. By four, he could hit a whiffle ball like nobody's business. He was largely ambidextrous, and I worked with him to encourage this. I had intended to do this with my youngest son as well. Then came Multiple Sclerosis.

I had done so much with my oldest boy. At three, he would go off the high dive, yes, in the deep end. He was fearless. I wanted to impart that sort of gravitas on both of my children, but one got all my attention until age seven, and the other was seemingly neglected because just as I was starting to focus more of my attention on him, I suddenly had to start worrying about myself.

Meanwhile, Sherri strapped in for the long haul. We all stand in front of our Maker and promise for better or worse. When you do so when we're young and beautiful and don't really understand the implication of such a proclamation, we glibly reply, "I do." Today, though, at some point, half of us don't. Fortunately for me, Sherri took her promise seriously. We're at thirty-six years and counting.

As for me, I quickly elected to put a brave face on it all. The path I'd chosen had locked me into, great though it was, a narrow conduit of existence. Now, I would be forced to find another way in life. All the things that I'd long ago put away in the attic of possibility could be explored once again. Vocations once dreamed, the things that had been trampled by my ravenous passion for flying and fighting in the sky, were now suddenly available. I thought about business and finance and believed this was to be my next passion. High finance appealed to me, having studied economics in undergraduate school. I'd originally started down the path of Naval Aviation as the first step toward greatness. Now having become thoroughly addicted to flying fighters in the Navy, I viewed the impediment of MS as both a blessing and a curse. It was a curse because it stopped me from ever flying again. What an idiot. It was a blessing because it would force me to renew my focus on world domination. What an idiot. I decided that my next logical step was a career in finance, where I would quickly achieve vast wealth. What an idiot. I started to study for the GMAT.

"The grass," as they say, "is always greener." My interests are eclectic, to say the least. When I lived on a ship, during downtimes, I studied for and passed my Series 7. That is correct. You read that correctly. I may have been the only Navy Fighter Pilot in the fleet with a valid stockbroker's license. While others were reading books on my second cruise, I started writing one. Yet, I'd been unable to fully cultivate my wide and varied interests because my true passion, flying tactical jets, demanded the bulk of my time.

Thus, honing my flying skills was my chief concern. I loved flying and fighting the jet. I could not believe they were paying me for it. I can only liken it to an illicit drug. The more you do it, the more you want to do it. I believed it to be the source of my happiness. Now the "salad days" were over. Our quest for happiness often supplants our natural inclination toward righteous living, the very thing that—given a chance—ultimately results in our happiness.

Sadly, in my desperate search to fill this sudden and cavernous void, I would stumble along a broken road of shattered dreams seeking something else to fill that empty space. It only took me fifteen years to discover what that "something" was.

I wasn't about to go down without a fight. After my initial exacerbation, I didn't feel that bad. Maybe it wasn't MS?

I remember pulling the carcass of a Mule deer down a mountainside as the sun came up. When the sun was high enough—to my horror—I discovered that the animal's body was crawling with ticks. That little incident had happened a few years earlier. Perhaps I was suffering from Lyme Disease?

The reason that Navy Medicine and Naval Aviation were rooting for something other than Multiple Sclerosis was that if my issues were caused by some other culprit, Lyme Disease, Guillain-Barré Syndrome, or some other treatable malady, I might eventually fly again. At this stage, it started to dawn on me that the doctors were on my side. That seemed strange. For nearly a decade, I had been flying on a Medical Waiver that had been granted—by the skin of my teeth—way back when we lived in Pensacola. That waiver had only been lifted a year or two earlier.

I spent the next several months getting poked, prodded, and evaluated. At this point, Medical experts had ruled out nearly every other possibility. Yet, although they had managed to eliminate a plethora of ailments, they were reluctant to officially diagnose Multiple Sclerosis. That's because, after spinal taps, MRIs, and a myriad of other tests, there was nothing additional to indicate MS. Moreover, I'd had no exacerbations since the first one that had started on Thanksgiving Day months earlier.

After several months and much fervent deliberation, it was determined that I would be allowed to fly again. I was ecstatic. It was all that I thought mattered in life.

I completed an abbreviated syllabus at the Fleet Replacement Squadron at NAS Lemoore down in California's San Joaquin Valley. A month later, I was back in Fallon. I was still the Fleet Liaison Officer at the Naval Strike and Air Warfare Center, and eventually, I got to fly intercepts at night versus all the carrier air wings as they came through to sharpen their swords before deployment.

I was flying again, but I had spent nearly two years in Limbo. I was marking time in the hope of making it back out to the fleet.

Then I had another exacerbation. I was forced to make peace with the notion that I would never lead a squadron over the horizon into harm's way. It was, I imagine, like losing a limb.

Yet, I am a glass-half-full kind of person. I'm certain people even today confuse my ebullience with ignorance. I know there was plenty of both. It was all about coming to grips, albeit slowly, with the end of what was finally shaping up to be a promising career. I started to peek over the fence to spy the boundless horizon of what lay beyond.

In nineteen ninety-seven, I expressed a desire to get to the bottom of my medical issues. It didn't take long before I was officially diagnosed with Multiple Sclerosis. The Navy offered me other opportunities, none very realistic or appealing. After a decade of flying fast movers, every other alternative seemed utterly feckless.

I was fast approaching the end of my career. Aily died that spring. People who've never owned a pet will say it's like losing a member of the family. Of course, if you've ever had a good dog, you know full well that they *are* a member of your family. My sister always says, "God spelled backward." That's not quite right, though. They're one of God's many gifts. Constant, faithful, loving, and infinitely kind, they teach us the best traits of what it means to be human. Perhaps the saddest lesson they teach us is that life is short, so don't waste a second on that which is petty. Love like there is no tomorrow.

My last hurrah in the Navy came when NSAWC's Operations Officer scheduled me for a ride in one of our two-seat Hornets. He didn't have to do that, but "Trim" is a class act. By this time, I'd been Med-Down again for several months. I thought I'd never fly a tactical jet again in my life. On that day, I remember being a little nervous and excited.

It was another sunny day in the high desert when "Stitch" and I went wheels in the well. "Stitch" had shown up a year into my tour at NSAWC. Now he was giving me my last ride in a tactical airplane. He had been named the Strike-Fighter Junior Officer of the year, the same year I had been nominated.

Having flown around the operating area for nearly six years, I gave "Stitch" a detailed tour of the area. As a Bogey, my friends and I had simulated an enemy air force protecting its territory from "invading Yanqui Air Pirates." As such, we were intimately familiar with our simulated homeland.

For the last time in my life, I got to feel a little G. Too soon, we were in the break, and "Stitch" let me land one last time. I'd been a land-based bogey driver for so long that I flared, softly squeaking onto the runway like a danged airline pilot. I started to pull the throttles back to idle, but they inexplicably shot forward as the jet sprang back into the sky.

"No, no, you can't land like you're in the Air Force. Fly the ball. Land like you're coming aboard," Stitch said. "Four oh six, touch and go, is goin' around for one more pass," he radioed to the tower.

"Roger. Four oh six cleared. Proceed downwind," the tower answered.

Stitch was right, I thought. My last landing in a Navy jet, by God, should be a Navy landing. And so it was.

I wasn't quite finished, theoretically, at least. As a Fleet Liaison Officer, I spent a few days in Newport News, Virginia, where I was part of a working group for a new class of aircraft carriers, what is now the Gerald R. Ford-class. Back in Fallon, I got to participate in a tactical working group that recommended which prototype of the advanced tactical fighter should be selected, what is now known as the F-35 Lightning. Lastly, I flew out to the Nimitz to record results, evaluate, and report on the true sortie generation capabilities of an air wing conducting operations at sea. I reported directly to the Battlegroup Commander, a two-star admiral.

I spent a couple of weeks in Saudi Arabia, in July no less, helping a joint planning group plan an airstrike that never happened. Good times, not.

That all said, my career was dwindling to its inevitable close. The Detailers in Tennessee had offered me a Public Affairs Officer Position. Yet that meant starting over in a job where my level of expertise was nil.

Mainly, though, it wasn't the military that I loved; it was flying. I wanted to be a fighter pilot. That required me to be a military officer. Now flying was no longer an option.

I thought it was high time to go out and conquer the real world. I'd taken the GMAT and, as per normal, recorded a score that was ever so slightly above average. Okay, Stanford and Harvard were out, but I thought it best to go back home anyhow.

I checked out on terminal leave on Thirty June Nineteen Ninety-Eight and headed East. I pulled into my dad's driveway twenty-seven hours later. I was back in Iowa for my first civilian job interview.

Sherri and the boys were still in Nevada. After the interview, I flew back commercially, and since we had three cars, she and I would caravan back across I-80. It was the end of the idyllic life we had known.

me to be a military officer. Now flying was no longer an option.

I thought it was high time to go out and conquer the real world. I'd taken the GMAT and, as per normal, recorded a score that was ever so slightly above average. Okay, Stanford and Harvard were out, but I thought it best to go back home anyhow.

I checked out on terminal leave on Thirty June Nineteen Ninety-Eight and headed East. I pulled into my dad's driveway twenty-seven hours later. I was back in Iowa for my first civilian job interview.

Sherri and the boys were still in Nevada. After the interview, I flew back commercially, and since we had three cars, she and I would caravan back across I-80. It was the end of the idyllic life we had known.

Chapter Sixteen:

Falling

My initial foray into finance, one would think, might have taken us to New York. That said, my home is Iowa. It is not widely advertised that Des Moines is an insurance capital of sorts. As such, there are more than a few places where investment jobs do exist. One of those was the job I'd interviewed for in early July. I went to work as a Portfolio Manager's Assistant for a large (then privately held) insurance company. More accurately, I worked for a subsidiary company, the investment arm of said company. I worked in the growth equity section tracking the daily performance of large, medium, and small-cap growth investments. It was equities, and it was an upwardly mobile position. I needed to attain either an MBA or CFA, and both were preferred. My goal was to work my way into an investment analyst position.

I began working for our Growth Style Portfolio Managers (PMs). I started my MBA at the University of Iowa. I began studying for level one of the CFA exam.

Initially, I confess that leaving the Navy under less than desirable circumstances left me with a huge chip on my shoulder. I'd landed a sort of dream job. I started as a Portfolio Manager's Assistant (PMA) but was soon promoted to Jr. Stock Analyst. A Buy-side Stock Analyst recommends stocks for the Portfolio Managers to buy for their respective portfolios. A Buy-side Stock Analyst living in Iowa can't make the serious dough that a Sell-side Analyst working for Merrill Lynch or some other major brokerage firm does. Yet with time, they are well compensated.

I had an unlimited travel budget to go visit the companies that I was pitching. Travel was not mandatory, though. I liked that flexibility. Most of the time was spent building financial models to justify one's price target for an individual name (stock). One of the main perks was when sell-side guys would come to town to wine and dine you and pitch their ideas, hoping that you would take up their cause and make their pitches your own. Sometimes you would go to investment conferences held in swanky hotels in New York or Phoenix or San Francisco, or Silicon Valley. Sometimes you would attend a training symposium held at one of the major brokerage houses, usually in New York. The company was also paying for the lion's share of my MBA.

Yet, despite falling into a nearly perfect gig, a fall is how I chose to perceive it. Oh, I kept a positive outlook and managed a brave face, but like Icarus, drowning seemed preferable.

It was a dream job—for anyone who loved finance. The problem was that I'd been a fighter pilot. Moreover, I'd been dabbling in finance since leaving undergraduate school, where I'd earned a double major in both Economics and Business Management. During the roaring nineties, I had made money in stocks and fancied myself an expert when it came to trading equities.

I began to discover that I wasn't truly passionate about the investment world. I wasn't in love with stocks. I was in love with the idea of stocks and what they represented. Most investment analysts love math and have a relatively high IQ. They aggressively scour their assigned universe to find any excess value. Moreover, by the time Y2k happened (a non-event), I'd come to the realization that I was no expert. I had no real love for math and nothing earth-shattering to share with the wider investment world. Any idiot could've made money in the nineties. Some of us did.

In no man's land, halfway to my MBA, with no significant wins to speak of, I decided my best bet was to lean in and press on. I worked ten hours a day and then went to class at night.

I was riding somewhere with my dad one weekend. We were on our way to get coffee or swing by the local hardware store. As we traveled, I regaled him with my long-range plans.

"I need to get my MBA. That'll take a couple more years. I need to finish my CFA, I've got levels two and three still to do, and that's going to take at least two years..."

"You know your kids are only young once," Dad said.

True wisdom. Too bad no one heard it.

"I know, but if I can do it, this is a tremendous opportunity," I said, thinking the old man didn't understand.

Around this time, I was approached to join the Knights of Columbus, a men's Catholic fraternal organization. Frankly, I'm not sure why I decided to join. I was, at best, a lukewarm practitioner of my religion. I signed up and paid my dues, but that was the extent of my involvement.

I began self-administered Intramuscular injections to curb the future progression of my disease. Stabbing yourself with a needle isn't for queasy or timid folk. But I was a fighter pilot, and if this was my new lot, I'd grin and bear it.

The ridiculous nature of my initial resistance to treatment began to manifest itself. I was becoming a little more unsteady on my feet, and the distance I could travel was continually diminishing. If memory serves, I still had the occasional dream where I could run. Rarer still, I would sometimes dream of flying, not flying like a bird or superman but flying a jet.

The point is although I was attempting to combat disease progression with one of the many treatments out there, my disease was, in fact, progressing. Moreover, while I spent nearly two years attempting to get cleared to fly again, my disease had quietly advanced unabated. It was around this time that I first noted the frequency of my exacerbations increasing.

From about the year 2000 to 2003, I was often on a regimen of steroids (read: Prednisone) to help minimize the effect of my exacerbations. We had built a house and moved back to our hometown. Sherri and I had originally decided to retire out west, but after my diagnosis—not knowing how my disease might progress—we thought it best to go home to Iowa to be near friends and family in case we needed support. We often do, by the way, and our family and friends always step up. It's awe-inspiring.

I was still working as a buy-side analyst and still working toward an MBA. I also began researching alternative treatments for my disease. A stem cell transplant seemed most promising.

I'd also taken and passed level one of the CFA (Certified Financial Analyst) exams. I'm told that level one, which is multiple-choice, is the easiest of the three exams necessary for qualification. I passed by the skin of my teeth. To this day, I consider it the most difficult exam I've ever taken. By the way, I've taken a few exams.

We were in a staff meeting one sunny September morning when one of the Office Assistants rushed in, obviously shaken, and announced that an airplane had crashed into the World Trade Center. No one knew what to make of this terrible calamity, but as the day wore on, it was soon appallingly clear.

I'd started the job intent on obtaining my MBA and CFA. I quickly realized that this was an unrealistic goal. I never possessed the intellectual chops to do post-graduate work in finance in two separate programs simultaneously. Moreover, I noticed the first signs of cognitive issues associated with Multiple Sclerosis. I knew that I'd have to pick one discipline, finish it, and then go back to the other. As a risk mitigation strategy of sorts, I chose to finish my MBA first, figuring that it would qualify me for a broader spectrum of careers. Happily, in December of 2003, I limped across the finish line and graduated from the Henry B. Tippie School of Management, University of Iowa. Go Hawks.

I was assisting with capital goods. I also covered airline stocks as well as defense names. If that wasn't enough, I tracked for-profit secondary education stocks. Our shop was steeped in a tradition of fundamental analysis. Our bread and butter was DCF (discounted cash flow), supplemented by other methodologies such as EVA, EPS, PE or PEG, Dividend Yield, Payout Ratio, etc. Additionally, one could avoid reinventing the wheel by simply pouring over the research of the sell-side analysts. All of this is an attempt to find the true intrinsic value of a stock. Yet, finding that diamond in the rough isn't so easy. There are thousands of analysts across the globe pouring over the balance sheets, income statements, 10k's, and annual reports of every publicly traded name out there. After nearly four years, I'd learned a lot but hadn't exactly distinguished myself as a budding financial guru.

Meanwhile, my disease was progressing. As mentioned, as I neared the end of my MBA, it was evident—to me at least—that MS was starting to have a noticeable impact on my cognitive abilities. Moreover, though I've not shared this until this moment, I noticed that I would cry at the drop of a hat and laugh like a braying donkey at any little witticism. PseudoBulbar Affect or PBA was starting to take hold of my emotions. I recall that Sherri's grandfather had passed around this time. At the funeral, my brother-in-law delivered a tremendous eulogy. Folks cried and laughed as they listened. After the ceremony, I tried to tell my brother-in-law what a fine tribute he'd given, but I couldn't get the words out. I soon found myself standing in front of him like a blubbering idiot, a river of tears pouring down my face.

I kept giving myself shots. There was little evidence that it helped, but neurologists kept pointing out that we don't know how bad it would be if you stopped. Fear prevailed, and I kept stabbing myself once a week. Without notice, life was slowly becoming a monotonous grind. It's shameful for me to think about it today. There are more than a few people my sons' ages ending it all because they see no way out of the darkness. Honestly, my own thoughts of suicide were fleeting. Oh, I'm sure I was depressed. Being forced out of the cockpit was indeed a bitter pill. But I was a long way from eating my gun. I admit thinking of driving into a bridge abutment from time to time but compared to some of our veterans today, people fighting real demons, like PTSD or TBI, I feel ashamed that I gave ending my life even a moment's consideration.

That said, my growing depression was real. Life as I had envisioned it was not panning out. My master plan, now derailed, was finally recognized for what it was, maybe what it had always been, a pipe dream. My "glass half full" attitude soon seemed ludicrous. I'd dropped my glass several miles back. I started showing up late to work. I slept a lot. If possible, I became more withdrawn from friends and family. Looking back, I can only shake my head at the level of my arrogance and ignorance. At this stage of my life, I sort of curled into a fetal position and nurtured an impressive "woe is me" attitude. I chose to look inward at my own maladies rather than out toward the triumph or tribulation of those around me.

At this stage of our lives, Sherri was essentially a single parent... again. I went from the frenetic existence of a budding "master of the universe" to folding like a cheap suit and curling into a fetal ball. Instead of my children, I nurtured the ever-growing black hole that was my future.

I'd finished my MBA (emphasis on finance) from the University of Iowa. Two months later—in February of 2004—I was let go from the job that many others (normal human beings, that is) would have loved.

I was a stock analyst at the investment arm of a major insurer. Travel was at my discretion. I could do as much or as little as my research demanded. It was upwardly mobile and would have eventually commanded an exceedingly comfortable salary. The people were competent and friendly. Yet I hated it. There were no jets to fly.

Now I was unemployed, and for the first time in my life, I started to question myself. Exactly what was I doing?

I had heard about a doctor in Chicago who was doing an experimental treatment for people suffering from Multiple Sclerosis. My dad and I drove out there for an appointment that I had been trying to get for months. I wondered if my job loss was part of some grand design. Sans job, I was free to go to the appointment at Northwestern Hospital in Chicago. Moreover, I was suddenly free for the procedure, which would last for several weeks.

The treatment would entail a stem cell transplant. The doctor explained it to me. The more I heard, the more I knew this was for me. Theoretically, it would arrest the onset of further disability. By this time in my life, I could not walk more than a mile or two, running was a distant memory, and I'd started to notice a small cognitive deficit.

"I'm absolutely certain that our treatment could help you," the doctor said.

"How much does it cost, and does insurance cover any of it?" I asked.

The doctor's smile dampened briefly, and then he said, "Remember, this procedure is still experimental. As such, most insurance companies will not cover it."

"How much?" my dad asked.

"Two-fifty to five hundred."

"Thousand?" I asked, already knowing the answer.

The doctor gave a quick nod but then continued, "Most of our patients will do a series of fundraisers in order to generate the necessary amount, and we don't require the full cost upfront." He then gave several examples of success stories—not so much for the procedure—but of various fundraising triumphs. He concluded with, "Again, you're a nearly perfect candidate, we've demonstrated the efficacy of this procedure, and we could start on Monday. All we need is seventy thousand dollars."

"It sounds very promising, Doc, but I don't have seventy K lying around. Let me consider some fundraising ideas and get back to you." With that, we went back to Iowa.

Initially downtrodden, I did not stay that way long. Where there's a will and all. On the way home, a plan emerged. I was now medically retired military. I would get the government to pay for it.

We were just across the Mississippi when a friend from Grad School called with a job offer.

In February of 2004, I started working as a Risk Analyst for a regulated utility firm in my home state. There was a lot to learn. The people, though not the sort of extroverts I'd encountered in both of my previous jobs, were welcoming.

I began tracking the prices of Natural Gas and Electricity. Later I added coal to my repertoire. I learned about basis, and transport, about peak and off-peak electricity, I learned where Henry Hub was, the Permian Basin, and the significance of the Powder River Basin.

The Risk Department did not evaluate or track operational risk. Our focus was purely associated with financial risk. We tracked the sales and purchases of natural gas and electricity and ensured that those transactions did not exceed management's prescribed limits.

Initially, I tried to hit the ground running. I really did. I worked ten hours a day for a year. Slow but sure, things started making sense. That said, every so often, things would not go well, and occasionally twelve, fourteen, even sixteen-hour days, though rare, were not unprecedented. When things went awry, the cause was often self-induced. It was evident to me that I was, at times, struggling with some of the more complex issues associated with my job. Prior to MS, in case you haven't discerned it already, I was never the "sharpest knife in the drawer." I would typically make up for any intellectual disparity by working harder than the next guy. Now, however, I was coming to recognize that the harder I worked, the more I struggled with cognitive issues. And the more I struggled with cognitive issues, the harder I had to work. Caught in this terrible death spiral, I knew that something would eventually have to give.

At this juncture, I was still living in the closet with respect to my disease. The fear, not wholly unfounded, was that companies would be reluctant to hire someone with a known neurological malady. ADA, or the Americans With Disabilities Act, in theory, prohibits companies from refusing to hire or fire an employee based solely on a person's disability. The reality, however, is that companies know this and will find other ways to justify such action.

So began my quest to hide in plain sight. I'd been truthful about pretty much everything. Yet when asked why I sometimes seemed to walk with a limp, I would pass it off as an old football injury that got re-injured early in my time in the military. That wasn't exactly a lie, but it certainly wasn't the truth. The truth was that my knee had not bothered me in years. MS was the reason I moved like a wounded duck.

I'd been an athlete for much of my early life. One of my coworkers, a natural gas trader, kept a small football at his desk, and he would often chuck it to fellow co-workers on the trading floor. Fortunately, Risk was down on the other end of the trading floor. By now, MS had pretty much ravaged my hand-eye coordination. The once graceful prowess of an athlete had been replaced by the spastic uncertainty of a toddler. The problem was that the nearest restroom required an advance past NG. Compounding the issue, multiple sclerosis influences one's bathroom habits. Increased frequency and urgency had already figured prominently in my life.

Each trek to the bathroom involved transit through the natural gas area where—at least so far as maintaining secrecy—there was the very real risk that I would hear the words "think quick" and look up to see a tiny football spiraling toward me. I always prayed silently as I moved quickly toward the restrooms, head down, that my secret would not be inadvertently revealed. It wasn't... at least not that way.

I was returning a book at the local library one afternoon. It was a sunny summer day. I had just gotten back into my vehicle when my phone started to ring. It was from Washington, D.C.

"Yes, May I speak with Lieutenant Commander Geneser?"

"Speaking."

"Hello, this is Ms. Martin with the Veterans Administration."

"Yes, ma'am?"

"We've decided to fund your stem cell transplant."

Nice, I thought. Imagining fall in the "windy city." "That's very good news. When will I be going out to Chicago?"

"Chicago?"

"Yes, the program is at Northwestern Hospital."

"Yes, well, we're going to pay for a stem cell transplant, but not in Chicago. There are two facilities within the Veterans Administration where stem cell transplants happen on a regular basis."

"For MS?" I asked, reeling at the blasé attitude of this pencil pusher.

"No. Typically, it's for various forms of cancer, but a stem cell transplant is a stem cell transplant. We can do this. And if you want us to pay for it, there are only two places in the country where the VA performs them."

"Where's that?"

"Tennessee or Washington state."

"Where at in Washington?"

"Seattle."

Darkness had enveloped me like a cloaking device. It had essentially rendered me invisible. The me that I had wanted to become would never be. Coming to grips with that fact was frightful. While I sat around wrapped in a cocoon of self-pity, my children grew, mainly without a father. Oh, I was there, taking up space mostly. Yet, I was disengaged from my children, more like a piece of furniture than a father.

At first, I was busily chasing my new career. Then it was my MBA. Finally, I just sort of gave up. My endless descending spiral had my entire family hurtling toward oblivion.

Now I wasn't even going to be there physically. Worse still, traveling with me out to Seattle was the only fully engaged parent my boys still had.

I had to come clean at work. I never out and out lied about my condition. I just never shared the whole truth. I'd skillfully avoided discussing my health issues since leaving the Navy but explaining my health-related leave of absence required full candor. I'm not sure how management felt, but they handled the news gracefully. I got my ducks in a row. I worked with my boss and co-workers to ensure that all my daily responsibilities were covered. I signed up for Family Medical Leave (FMLA).

On November thirteenth, we flew out to Seattle. Our children were then fifteen and twelve.

They call it the Emerald City for a reason. It's so green. Upon arrival at SeaTac, we soon discovered why. It gets plenty of water. It rains there ten months out of the year.

The Puget Sound Veterans Administration Medical Center serves veterans in Seattle, Washington, and throughout the Pacific Northwest. Moreover, their proximity to the Seattle Cancer Care Institute (SCCI)—the place where the first stem cell transplant was performed—makes it one of two facilities in the VA system where bone marrow and stem cell transplants are routinely done.

As I've previously mentioned, an autologous stem cell transplant isn't cheap. If the Veterans Administration had not funded the procedure, we would not have spent months in Seattle.

Therein lies the problem, during the procedure, I would obviously not be working. Nor would Sherri. What's more, the cost of living in Seattle, Washington is slightly higher than in Des Moines, Iowa.

Despite the Veteran Administration's generosity, finances were still going to be tight. We would essentially be operating two households—one in a relatively high cost of living area. That is why, before leaving Iowa, we ran a fundraiser that generated slightly more than four thousand dollars. There is a long list of people, friends, relatives, guys from my time in the Navy, people from the surrounding communities, as well as members of both churches in my hometown. That stipend, seemingly meager when pitted against the cost of living in Seattle for nearly four months, somehow turned out to be just the right amount.

Chapter Seventeen:
Puget Sound

The fourth floor of the VA hospital in Seattle is called the Bone Marrow Transplant Unit (BMTU). The name was given when, years earlier, bone marrow transplants were considered cutting-edge medical technology. By the time we showed up, most of what happened on the fourth floor were stem cell transplants.

The initial step was meeting the doctors, nurses, and staff. Each, in turn, explained a different phase of the procedure. There were numerous briefings with nearly everyone involved in the process. At the very end is an explanation of all the risks. There are many things, and listing them all would be a bore. The biggest risk is, of course, death.

The simple man's explanation of a stem cell transplant, at least how I think of it, is like a hard restart for your computer. Many who have survived the experience will celebrate a new birthdate. One's immune system is brought down to near zero—in medical circles, this is referred to as a neutropenic state. This is what makes a stem cell transplant inherently dangerous. But of course, as any self-respecting fighter pilot would say, "danger is my middle name," to which a discriminating gentle reader might say BULL SHIT. Seriously, though, when severely neutropenic, any common little virus or bacteria can and often does kill. That is because the body's immune system is essentially nonexistent. In this severely compromised state, a common cold is often a death sentence. That is why when you are most vulnerable, you are isolated in a positively pressurized room. Visitors are discouraged. Nurses and caregivers are not allowed to enter if they suspect the onslaught of a sniffle.

A day after I signed my acknowledgment of risk, I began a regimen of G-CSF (Growth Colony Stimulating Factor). A drug known as filgrastim was given to boost the production of stem cells. Subcutaneous injections were given on a regular basis to stimulate the bone marrow to produce such a huge abundance of stem cells that they end up in one's bloodstream. This overabundance is then harvested and frozen for eventual reintroduction.

First, the body must undergo a conditioning phase. This is an innocuous way of saying that I began a regimen of chemotherapy designed to kill your immune system.

From a timeline perspective, my stem cells were harvested on November 30th, 2005. Chemotherapy commenced on December 9th, 2005, and continued until December fifteenth. My Stem Cells were re-infused on that day. Many who have undergone a stem cell transplant celebrate this as a second birthday.

Forgive the shameless plug but for a more detailed account, check out my first attempt to chronicle the procedure in my abbreviated memoir, *The Gift.* It is available in digital format everywhere.

For the next several days, I waited in my pressurized hospital room on the fourth floor of the Puget Sound Veterans Hospital for my white blood cell count to rise to a level that would allow me to safely roam among my fellow human beings.

As Christmas loomed, my hometown's American Legion Post flew our boys out for the holiday. After the Navy, I was still fighting my own demons and chasing my own dreams. I didn't have time for an organization like the American Legion. I thought I had bigger fish to fry. So, the unrequited compassion of an organization I had thoroughly discounted nearly moved me to tears. Watching the reunion of Sherri and her boys after a month-long separation was indeed a privilege to witness.

While my kids were with us in Seattle, the docs started letting me out of the hospital on a limited basis. That is also when my hair started falling out. The boys went back to Iowa a few days after Christmas. Soon after, I left the hospital as an inpatient but moved into the two-room efficiency apartment where my chief caregiver (Sherri) lived. By then, I was as bald as a cue ball.

Alien and his family hail from the Pacific Northwest, and we spent a few weekends at their home catching up and eating Tillamook® ice cream. He even took me fishing in his drift boat once.

In mid-February, Sherri swapped out caregiver duties with my mother-in-law. I took her to the top of the Space Needle for lunch. We boarded the ferry out to Bremerton to see the ship I once lived on, then mothballed. In mid-March, we could leave.

I remember the good stuff, such as Tillamook® ice cream, my boys visiting, fighting a big King Salmon as we floated down an aspen-cloaked river, my caregivers, Sherri chief among them, the restaurant at the top of the Space Needle. But I also remember that four or five people died in the BMTU while I was there.

Here's the main thing with respect to an autologous stem cell transplant for Multiple Sclerosis: before my trip to Seattle, I gave myself shots to combat the symptoms of MS. At various times Neurologists had me on most of the different MS medications in existence at that time. Yet my exacerbations had continually increased in both frequency and severity. Before Seattle, I had an exacerbation about every ninety days. After my stem cell transplant—now fifteen years ago—I take no MS. medications, and I've had one minor MS exacerbation since 2006.

Admittedly, I'm a sample size of one, and as such, my results are statistically insignificant. Yet more than twenty years have passed since my official diagnosis, and I'm still ambulatory.

Chapter Eighteen:

Continued Plummet

I went back to work. For a couple of years, things were okay. It was already well established that I was the least intelligent Risk Analyst at the company. The guy I sat by was a CPA and the other guy in my immediate area, like me, also had his MBA. I'd known it before I left for Seattle. I had jumped into the intellectual deep end without my floaties.

Moreover, I could see no path for advancement. I was stuck in what I perceived as a dead-end job where there was no clear path to advance. You know what they say, "perception is reality." As such, whether advancement was an actual possibility, who knows? With every passing year of lackluster performance, my enthusiasm waned, and options dwindled.

I looked at my chances of moving into some other line of work within the company. Yet, I was never bold enough to try. I think that during my time there, I may have applied internally for two other positions in eleven years. With one, I never heard back. With the other, an offer was, in fact, made, but for lack of gumption (read: fear of the unknown), I turned it down.

So, not only was my performance subpar, but I did not find the work itself particularly interesting. Recall that my interest in finance had put me on a track that would limit my choices to jobs much like the one I currently held. Sometimes I wondered if—all those years ago, just out of undergrad—I should have taken the bank job. Instead, I compare every job, including the one I was in, to that of Assistant Ops in VFA-127. Nothing could ever measure up. My life had been hurtling down a steep mountain for some time. I was racing from a lofty peak toward the canyon floor, now not so far below.

It became intuitively obvious to me that my survival as a Risk Analyst depended solely on my ability to blend in and not get noticed. I did my work as best I could, which was usually, though not always, acceptable. I seldom volunteered for extra duty. I was afraid that additional projects might highlight my limitations. They were soon recognized anyhow, despite my best efforts to conceal them. It was indeed a quandary. Volunteering for special projects would increase the risk of a mistake, thus underscoring my intellectual deficits. Avoiding them shined a beacon on the lack of confidence I had in my innate abilities.

And so, the long slog continued. From the time I returned in the spring of 2006 until my untimely departure in the summer of 2015, I worked hard to avoid hard work. During that decade, I impressed neither co-workers nor supervisors. Raises based upon individual performance were like unicorns on the freeway. Remuneration was less than any MBA worth a damn would have acquiesced to accept. More importantly, I was doing work that I did not find stimulating. Looking back, did I suck because I hated my job, or did I hate my job because I sucked? The more important question was, why did I stay in a job that I hated for more than a decade? In a word, fear.

I was worried that finding a new career for a middle-aged man with MS would be onerous at best. Hindsight tells me that this fear—something a fighter pilot is loath to admit—was somewhat exaggerated. Maybe, maybe not. After all, in 2008, when the financial world was imploding, I worked for a regulated utility firm in the Midwest. I had a decent-paying job that was comparatively secure.

Meanwhile, my home life continued to suffer. I had finished school. I had more time at home, yet my boys did not need me. They never asked me for advice. When they had really needed me to step up, I wasn't there. "You know your kids are only young once," my dad had said over a decade earlier when I was still hell-bent on becoming a master of the universe. Now, too late, I finally understood.

A combination of selfishness and vainglory conspired to render me something I'd never seen before: a bad dad. My own dad had always been there for me. To this day, I can't recall a time when he wasn't. Admittedly the trajectory of my life had been severely affected by a serious game-changer, Multiple Sclerosis. Yet, as I've previously alluded to, I thought it an opportunity to excel in some other walk of life.

By the time I was halfway through my stint as a Risk Analyst, I figured something big was just around the corner. One of my manuscripts would become the next "it" novel, win a Pulitzer, the screenplay, which I would advise on, would win an Oscar. Or maybe one of my entrepreneurial ventures would capture the attention of Mark Cuban or some other captain of industry. For those keeping score at home, none of these things have happened. The reality is that for many more years, my race toward oblivion would continue.

In 2013, I flew down to Atlanta for my best man's fiftieth birthday party. Carlos is my fraternity brother and was best man at our wedding. His little brother Ricardo is my little brother in our fraternity. He, too, lives in Atlanta. I hadn't seen Carlos since his wedding in McAllen, Texas, in 1986. At that time, Sherri and I were stationed in Kingsville, Texas, where I flew T-2s.

My trip went off without a hitch... almost. Los and his wife, Teresa, run a first-class operation. His success in the corporate world doesn't surprise me. To say he's a people person is a gross understatement. The party was based on a Cuban theme. Mojitos were flowing, cigars were tested, and there was all manner of Cuban cuisine. It was a great evening. Carlos took me out to eat two or three times as well.

On the afternoon of my departure, we met Ricky for lunch. I offered to pay and pulled my wallet out. If memory serves, I don't think they let me pay, though.

Later that afternoon, while packing, I determined that my wallet was missing. Carlos had to drive all the way back to the restaurant to find my wallet. Things were going to be tight as the poor guy had to go almost downtown during rush hour. The last thing he said to me before he left was. "Don't try to move your luggage by yourself."

All I had was a carry-on. All I had to do was get it down the stairs, which, if I went slow, would be no problem. I took my time, and indeed it was no problem.

Of course, leaving my wallet at the restaurant was the sort of scatter-brained stuff that happened all too frequently in my life post-MS. I stepped out into the garage as Carlos had found my wallet and was not far from home.

Multiple Sclerosis has wreaked havoc on my balance. I always maintain three points of contact when I take a shower. The step was only about two inches in height, and as I stepped down holding my luggage, I only had two points of contact. I came off a two-inch step somewhat stiff-legged. My Tibia shattered when my heel contacted the cement floor. I fell and banged the back of my head on the cement. It hurt, but apparently, my skull is still as thick as ever. I tried to stand up but soon determined this wasn't possible. I'd never broken a bone, but the pain was pronounced. I have pretty high pain tolerance, but standing was out of the question. Carlos and Teresa's daughter, then in eighth grade, sat with me on the garage floor until her dad came home.

X-rays showed that I'd broken the top of my tibia. Carlos took me to the nearest emergency room, and Ricky met us there to check on me. "It takes a village," and it pains me to say that sometimes I'm more of a bother than an unruly toddler. That said, my true friends don't seem to mind the hassle. Though mortified, it's always a privilege to watch the grace and kindness of others.

I spent two more days in Atlanta. Carlos and Teresa were most gracious, and I had some serious painkillers. I can see how a guy might get hooked. That said, when Carlos eventually dropped me off at Atlanta-Hartsfield, I'm pretty sure he was glad to be rid of me.

The architect of my demise as a Risk Analyst was diligent in the dark arts of sabotage. Slowly, with painstaking precision and ruthless determination, the seeds of my destruction were sown. Then in the summer of 2015, the final spring in the complex machine was sprung. Who was responsible? It was one evil person. Me. But I'm getting ahead of myself.

Over the years, I became more efficient at my daily chores. As I improved, there were more hours to fill in each day. Since I'd decided long ago to keep my head down and not volunteer for any extra assignments, I spent idle time looking busy. Looking busy is boring. I began researching other non-work-related projects. As the years accumulated, I got to read about my dismal performance in annual performance reviews. In 2014, I received a disciplinary letter detailing my growing penchant for surfing the net on company time and equipment. By that time, big brother was watching every click of my mouse. Knowing this, I refrained from surfing for a time. It was a dark time. None of my dreams were coming true. My job, the third in an ever-descending spiral of nowhere vocations, was hanging by a thread.

Chapter Nineteen:
The Summons

A long time ago, when I was still in undergraduate school, or maybe even high school, my dad told me about the one religious retreat he had made in his life. It was called Cursillo.

"I think every Catholic man should go to at least one retreat in his life," he added. Dad is not an overtly religious man. He's always been a "last guy in, first guy out" kind of Sunday worshiper. That said, he is well-grounded in his Christian faith and in church doctrine, and, unlike his son's approach to child-rearing, he was hands-on when it came to teaching Christianity to his children.

So, at age fifty-one, after much arm twisting and incessant advertising after Masses, I signed up for a retreat called Christ Renews His Parish (CRHP). It was the first one held at my Parish. As far as it went, getting that check in the block, achieving that challenge, that rite of passage established by Dad so long ago was intriguing, nothing more. I'd had a world to conquer. MS changed that.

At zero seven, fifty-five, I stood at the door with my friend Dave, trying to decide whether to enter.

"Ya know, I've been sittin' in my truck for half an hour tryin' to decide if I really wanna do this," Dave said as we stood there staring at the door.

"I know. A whole weekend. Brutal, right?"

"Well, I'll go if you go," Dave said.

"Safety in numbers," I said as I pulled my carry-on across the threshold.

Today I sometimes wonder what my life would have been like had I not gone through the door that morning. I can tell you that it hasn't been the same since.

Way back in 2006, in my memoir, *The Gift*, I wrote the following: "Through MS, I've been gently cajoled down a very different path than I ever envisioned. Without making you puke, I hope you've been convinced that life, not despite MS but because of it, is a gift."

Way back then, I understood that Multiple Sclerosis was the major change agent in my life. My callsign is Sneezer, but it should've been Moto, for I am a master of the obvious. The thing is, back then, while I recognized that MS was the catalyst fomenting great change in my life, I didn't comprehend the utter metamorphosis that was about to happen that day in 2013.

The program began with breakfast. I suppose the embarrassing abundance of food that day and the next—provided by behind-the-scenes volunteers—was meant to encourage the less pious among us to stick it out for the weekend. The food alone was worth it, but the main course was food for the soul.

As the day wore on, it became intuitively obvious that someone at each table was part of the team. In turn, they would give testimony that pertained to some biblical concept. Attendees were given a bible as well as a general outline of events. Each table then had discussion time after each witness. Then there were activities for each table to further highlight the theme of that testimony.

One of the first things I noted was that most of the men, who were later revealed as presenters, were quite successful, according to human standards. Yet none assigned any special significance to it. Without ever mentioning it, their example served as a stark contrast to how I'd chosen to approach life. I'd always been highly acquisitive and, truth told, downright greedy. My materialistic, self-indulgent behavior was effectively masked by my limited means. Long ago, my long-range plan was to recreate my own version of Camelot. Yet, these gentlemen were operating on a different plane of existence. To a man, they demonstrated righteous prioritization of what was truly important, seeking first the wisdom of God.[41] As such, they had been most fortunate in other walks of life.

The other thing I noted was that every testimony was an amazing tale of God's grace manifest in each man's life. By lunchtime, I understood the bravery necessary to show that sort of vulnerability to others in the room. I noted the fact that each table had a box of Kleenex and that guys were frequently reaching for them. I came to understand that this pouring out of self was a great gift given freely by those presenting, a priceless gift for us all. It was just after we had gotten back from lunch that I finally came to believe that the Holy Spirit had joined us.

---

[41] But seek first the kingdom of God and His righteousness, and all these things will be provided for you. (Matthew 6:33)

So, it went throughout the rest of the day—each testimony more amazing than the one preceding it. The day ended with confession, followed by a late mass. I had not partaken in the sacrament of reconciliation in nearly a quarter of a century. I recall a night when I was heading down the passageway on the ship, and a priest was hearing the confession of a sailor right out in the passageway. I'll never forget the scene, the priest making the sign of the cross over the sailor's bowed head as I passed. What the sailor knew way back then was how good it felt to be cleansed. "Jesus did not leave us orphans."[42]

After we had finished, a small cadre of men, attendees, and presenters, were having a snack in the kitchen. We were all just standing around discussing the day's events when a man named Joe asked, "Now that you've seen this, what's next?"

"Next?" I said. "What do you mean?"

"You ought to think about joining the Knights of Columbus."

"Joe, I am a Knight. I've probably been a Knight longer than you," I said, feeling rather smug.

"Well, Kendall, I've been a Knight for six years. How come I've never seen you at a meeting?"

Those listening had a chuckle. I smiled and laughed at Joe's not-so-subtle challenge, but inside I was thinking, 'Hmm, he may have a point.'

Soon after, we all trundled off to bed. I did not sleep a wink. I considered what Joe had said to me and knew that my life had to change.

---

[42] Scott Hahn, "Swear To God," pg. 49

When I was a Knight, a Black Knight flying Tomcats in VF-154, I always had trouble with the beatitudes. What kind of fighter pilot cottons to the idea that "the meek shall inherit the earth?"[43] I mean, really. Honestly, have you ever known a fighter pilot? Meek is not the first word that comes to mind.

I was introduced, or more accurately reintroduced, to the beatitudes on the CRHP retreat (called "chirp" for short, even though the acronym said phonetically would be crhip). The idea of "meekness" was always a tough pill for me to swallow. Yet, let us consider the matter further. Fighter pilots, soldiers, policemen, or anyone going downrange may want to pay attention. Jesus Christ, Emmanuel, the King of Kings, the Lamb of God, described himself as "meek" on more than one occasion. He also made a whip to drive money changers out of the temple.[44] Sound meek? Initially, I did not "drink the Kool-Aid®," but instead of dismissing the notion out of hand or simply ignoring it like the good "cafeteria Catholic" I had always been, I decided this conundrum deserved further consideration. Fr. John Riccardo, a mesmerizing Catholic Radio personality, points out that "meek" actually means controlled strength. For

---

[43] The Eight Beatitudes of Jesus: 1) "Blessed are the poor in spirit, for theirs is the kingdom of Heaven. 2) Blessed are they who mourn, for they shall be comforted. 3) Blessed are the meek, for they shall inherit the earth. 4) Blessed are they who hunger and thirst for righteousness, for they shall be satisfied. 5) Blessed are the merciful, for they shall obtain mercy. 6) Blessed are the pure of heart, for they shall see God. 7) Blessed are the peacemakers, for they shall be called children of God. 8) Blessed are they who are persecuted for the sake of righteousness, for theirs is the kingdom of Heaven." Matthew 5:3-10

[44] John 2:15-16

instance, meeking a horse did not mean to strip the animal of its power but rather to harness the horse's tremendous strength so that it could be used as its master intended. Our modern-day definition of the word "meek," with synonyms like humble, timid, submissive, gentle, weak, cowed, and fearful, is severely skewed. In the time of Jesus, in either Greek or Aramaic, the word meant disciplined, controlled strength. Scholars surmise that Jesus used the term to indicate that despite his awesome power, he was always submissive to the will of his heavenly father, as we all should be. With that understanding, a successful fighter pilot is meek, as a disciplined application of awesome power is what they do.

With more than half a century in the rearview mirror, I started to fathom that perhaps I was being meeked. Maybe instead of my will, my future would hinge on the will of God.

By the time CRHP ended on Sunday afternoon, my life had changed. I was on fire.

Yet the long slog that is life continued. John Mellencamp may have said it best. "Life goes on, long after the thrill of livin' is gone."[45] My children were now grown. My oldest son had gone off to a Junior College to try and play baseball. Unfortunately, his heart wasn't in it. As a freshman, he got injured just prior to his school's southern trip. As a result, he was cut from the team. It saddens me, but the true reality is that best case, although he could have played somewhere in

[45] "Jack & Diane" is a 1982 hit rock song written and performed by American singer-songwriter John Mellencamp, then performing as "John Cougar." It appears on Mellencamp's album American Fool.

college, baseball was not his favorite sport. He made it through junior college. After receiving his associate degree, he said, "Dad, I don't really know what I want to do. I'd like to take a semester off. I'll go up to Iowa State when I figure it out." That was eleven years ago. His maternal grandfather, a great man that I think of almost daily—he passed in 2008—always said that his oldest grandson should look for something in the skilled trades. My oldest has been employed in a variety of building trades ever since he left school.

My youngest son—the one that had been essentially neglected after my diagnosis—decided that he wanted to join the military. By the time I attended CRHP, my youngest had been in the Army for three years.

Like his father, my youngest planned to make a career in the military. Initially, he, too, courted the Marine Corps. In high school, he had torn a labrum wrestling and, as such, required surgery. The USMC would not take him because of that little scar. We fought to get him in. We worked on a waiver via a hometown Vietnam Veteran in conjunction with Marine Sergeant Major Bradley Kasal. At the time, Sergeant Major Kasal[46] was a local recruiter stationed near our home. Despite the effort of such USMC heroes, my son was disqualified because of his shoulder. He immediately called the US Army.

My youngest, who'd a thunk it, wanted to be an operator in the thick of things. Yet, as an enlisted infantryman, this meant that he would be more in the thick of things than I ever was. I found myself in a bit of a quandary. As a former military officer, I could not

---

[46] Sergeant Major Bradley Kasal won the Navy Cross for combat operations in Fallujah, Iraq in 2004. He is the Author of "No Man Left Behind."

rightly try to dissuade my son from military service. All the while, the father in me was quietly screaming, "NO!" My combat duty was largely theoretical. If the wars that I had prayed for so long ago continued, my son's involvement would not be theoretical at all. Careful what you wish for.

Like me, he spent time as an adversary. Of course, in the infantry world, red forces carried AK-47s and fired rubber-painted rounds.

Chapter Twenty

A Witness to Witness

"Character is destiny," said the Greek (Heraclitus of Ephesus, circa 5th or 6th century, B.C.), and, if so, that makes me extremely nervous. Yet, I know God is merciful. One of my boys was ending his tour in Germany. The other lived upstairs in my own home. Yet my communication with either of them was almost nil.

Back in our "salad days," our boys ate all their meals with us. We said "Grace" at every meal. Slowly but surely, Multiple Sclerosis coupled with a lifetime of selfish, superficial, and trivial pursuits conspired to relegate what should have been most important to tertiary status. Raising children is not a "set it and forget it" endeavor. There isn't an autopilot. Kids don't have self-driving capability. While I was off getting an MBA, while I was busy considering my own plight, my sons grew up.

I'm shooting for Heaven. Eternal bliss and all, but I know that I'll be lucky to spend less than a thousand years in Purgatory. That is because I checked out as a father when my kids needed me most. I can't really talk with either of them. I can make small talk with my youngest, who I see only sparsely. My oldest will talk with me only when inebriated. Which, thankfully, is less often than a year or two ago. Sadly, it reminds me of an old Harry Chapin[47] standard.

Neither of them attends church. When I was younger, I believed that they would find God in their own way. In their early lives, they watched us go to church, say grace, and do at least a smattering of the things that more pious families do. I thought our boys would eventually learn by my example. And in what is perhaps the saddest sentence in this entire book, maybe they did.

When we should have been taking meals together, I was working toward an MBA. I should have let them catch me reading the bible or with Rosary beads in my hand. In those days, I didn't do those things. Now that I'm older, I fret that my youngest son's strongest memory of me might be me, beer in one hand and cigar in the other, laughing at someone's raunchy joke at a party in someone's backyard. I wish I had a do-over, a chance to let them see that real men read the bible, real men pray every day, and real men are not afraid to admit that Jesus is their friend.

The idea that going to church on Sunday is optional in America is sad. I know. It sounds kind of preachy. After all, back in the day, my own church attendance was somewhat sporadic.

---

[47] Harry Forster Chapin (December 7, 1942 – July 16, 1981) was an American singer-songwriter, humanitarian, and producer best known for his folk rock and pop rock songs, one of his most famous the 1974 tunes, "Cats In The Cradle," which details the result of absentee fatherhood.

In the early church, if the Romans caught you worshiping, you would have a chance to explain yourself, and if you promised to cease and desist, you might get to live. Can you imagine our world today if it were filled with a fraction of that faith? Many early Christians chose to die for a noble purpose rather than live a life of disappointment. They refused to renounce their faith.

Thankfully, no one must physically die to go to church in America today. Yet, in the post-Christian western world in which we live, bravery is, in fact, a prerequisite. To simply announce that you are choosing Church over the soccer game or whatever's happening takes guts. What's more, depending on where you live in this world, a practicing Christian still risks bodily harm, even death.

"Blessed are you when they insult you and persecute you and utter every kind of evil against you because of me." Jesus, Matthew 5:11

In some parts of this world, Christians still risk their lives to practice their faith. Meanwhile, it's optional here. My own children have a rather apathetic attitude toward their religion. Sadly, they learned this from their parents.

Latin Rite Catholics are often asked by our Evangelical friends, "Were you born again?" to which a typical reply would be, "Yes, when I was baptized." Another question we get is "Have you been saved?" and the standard answer is something like, "Yes, in the year 30-33 AD at 3 pm local time on Calvary Hill." That said, though perhaps not in keeping with Church Doctrine, I do feel like after my first Christ Renews His Parish retreat, I was sort of born again or saved. I had received my sacraments, baptism, first communion, reconciliation, confirmation, and marriage, yet despite that, I felt like that weekend had changed my life. I came to realize that during the first fifty-one years of my life, I lived according to "my will," not His.

My Parish had set it up to run CRHP twice a year for men and twice a year for women. Presenters are ideally chosen from prior attendees after an evening of prayer and discernment. Unfortunately, in a relatively small parish, finding "new blood" for each weekend—as was originally intended—is problematic. As a result, many of the presenters (i.e., those giving testimony) were repeat performers. I had been a recipient of great grace at the first CRHP our church held. I became a giver of grace as—over the next few years—I would participate in six other CRHP weekends as a presenter. I quickly discovered that team formation was—though it seems impossible—even more amazing than the weekend I had attended originally. Most importantly, I discerned that one receives the grace that one gives. In giving, you receive.

In my insatiable quest for enduring happiness, I'd always looked to the next big thing, the next thrill. Now I had come to realize that for the last half-century, I'd not been remotely cognizant of what true happiness looks like.

Flying fighters was the ultimate pursuit of happiness, but it was ephemeral, an insatiable monster that always demanded more. It was fun while it lasted, but as soon as there was "weight on wheels," I began to think about the next mission. It sounds weird, but it took MS for me to learn that happiness isn't achieved by a successive parade of cheap thrills. Rather it is the result of righteous living.

Slowly but surely, my passion was changing. I was discovering that true happiness is not something you take; it's something you give.

I was as much of a sponge as my defective noggin would allow. It was probably after my second CRHP weekend that I started attending Knights of Columbus meetings on a regular basis. I'd been a Knight for many years in name only, but after Joe's challenge, I decided to take a more active role. It was a truly symbiotic relationship; Knights attended CRHP, and CRHP attendees became Knights. This was most certainly a cross-pollination project run by the Holy Spirit. The result was a true renewal of our little Parish. But it was not only the Knights of Columbus that benefited. Virtually all of the church's organizations were infused with a new ecumenical spirit as "Christ truly did renew His Parish" with many new CRHP brothers and sisters. It was a wonderful thing to witness.

While I was ever so tentatively gaining my footing on solid ground with respect to eternal issues, the slippery slope of my job continued. It continued, but as previously mentioned, it was a toboggan race toward the abyss. What was different was that I no longer cared.

After all, Jesus said,

"Therefore, I tell you, do not worry about your life, what you will eat [or drink], or about your body, what you will wear. Is not life more than food and the body more than clothing? Look at the birds in the sky: they do not sow or reap, they gather nothing into barns, yet your heavenly Father feeds them. Are not you more important than they?"—Matthew 6:25-26

The converse is an "honest day's work for an honest day's pay." Truth be told, though, I still had a giant chip on my shoulder, the one that said, 'hey, I was a Naval officer and a fighter pilot. Now I'm relegated to the career of quantitative minion.' Moreover, my passion was not, and had never been, in the work. I could find no joy in it. A more disciplined individual might have persevered. I had a family to support. In some respects, I felt as though I'd been stoically tolerant for over a decade. However, I had already started looking elsewhere.

"But seek first the kingdom [of God] and His righteousness, and all these things will be given you besides."—Matthew 6:33

My lackluster performance, coupled with my penchant for alternative pursuits during working hours, had resulted in official disciplinary letters from my manager. My performance reviews were, at best, slightly below, and at worst, well below average.

In the winter of 2014, we had a big ice storm, and getting to work was treacherous for someone with compromised stability. Yet, I made it from my car to the front door without incident. Later that day, while walking across the trading floor, I fell—no big deal. Though highly embarrassing, I'd just pop back up and shake it off. Yet when I started to get up, I could not. Pain like I'd only felt when I'd broken my leg prevented it. They carted me off to the hospital in an ambulance. I'd broken my hip.

Early in my disease, I'd been prescribed Prednisone—in huge doses. I discovered the benefits but also the short-term side effects of the drug. Now I was being introduced to what the doctors had originally neglected to mention. One of the primary long-term side effects of Prednisone is that it softens bones. I soon found out that, on the left side of my body, I had the bone density of a ninety-eight-year-old Japanese woman—osteoporosis on the left side and osteopenia on the right.

I have screws in my hip now, and physical therapy taught me how to avoid falls, or if I do, to fall on my stronger right side. I take lots of calcium now and, at risk of jinxing myself, several years have passed since I've broken a bone.

I started to harbor the sneaking suspicion that perhaps management wanted to get rid of me because of my disability, but the reality was that I'd given management every reason to ask me to leave. In June of 2015, they finally did.

The world from which I hail says that the philosophical change in my outlook could only be described as me finding Jesus, or some might say, "he got religion." Friends of a more evangelical persuasion might argue that I've been "born again." I don't want to freak any of my old friends out. I still laugh, and I still like a beer now and again, but truth be told, though it has been a life-long journey, I have found Jesus. I did get religion. I have been born again. It all began with what might be considered an unfortunate turn—Multiple Sclerosis.

My journey toward eternal life has continued in increments. Of course, the question we all must contemplate is where we will spend that eternity. Even though I am about seventy to ninety percent less capable by every measure today, I probably do seventy to ninety percent more for my fellow human beings.

Before you nominate me for sainthood, maybe I should share a little more detail. See, I'm certainly not out of the woods just yet. I have a lot to answer for.

I prayed for war. Many consider Sir Winston Churchill a modern-day savior of western civilization (he was, by the way). Many others consider him an opportunistic warmonger. "It is unquestionably true that Churchill loved war in this obvious sense, that without war, he knew that there could be no glory—no real chance to emulate Napoleon,"[48] or in my case Churchill.

"He knew how war and its risks had lifted men and painted everyday deeds with fame."[49] Therein lies my greatest sin, and there are many. Like Churchill, I emulated the daring deeds of great heroes who had gone before me, and I, too, needed a war to paint my "everyday deeds with fame."[50] After all, I originally wanted to build my own Camelot. And so, instead of praying for peace, as I do today, I prayed for war. God, in His infinite wisdom, would eventually grant my prayer. But I was spared the horrors of war, though that horror is admittedly rather opaque from thirty thousand feet. My youngest son, however, as an Army Infantryman, got to see it up close. He went to Afghanistan. Twice. Careful what you pray for. Alas, you may get it.

My spiritual advisor, Deacon Tom, equates spiritual awakening to that of walking through a door into a huge, ornate, and magical room. It is the most miraculous room you have ever been in, and you never want to leave. Yet, at the room's far end is another door. The point is there is always another door. The more you learn about Christianity, the more you realize how much

---

[48] Boris Johnson, "The Churchill Factor," pg. 169

[49] Ibid

[50] Ibid

you don't know (the next door). The question is, simply, do you have the courage and curiosity to open that next door? So now, that is what I do. I journey across the expanse of an amazing space, open the door and step across the threshold. I suspect that I'll be going through doors until I, God willing, reach paradise.

Speaking of opening that next door, I look back over the last few years and recall my friend Dave and I standing at the entrance of our first Christ Renews His Parish (CRHP) retreat, seriously considering whether to enter. Dave and I have attended seven weekends, five together. Although reticent that first day, the man has always been a pillar of faith in the parish, but after attending seven of the eight CRHPs in our little church, held between 2013 and 2016, Dave is an example for us all.

As previously mentioned, in June of 2015, I was asked to leave my post as a Risk Analyst. While this was a somewhat difficult pill to swallow, being an eternal optimist, I figured opportunity would fall like rain for a former Naval Officer with an MBA. However, such was not the case. While I may have possessed an impressive resume, I was a fifty-three-year-old man with Multiple Sclerosis. Moreover, I hadn't exactly set the world on fire since becoming a civilian. In fact, the trajectory of my life after the military was a rather sad and continuous shallow plummet toward obscurity.

Yet, the remnant of a pervading narcissism remained. Looking back, I felt like the world still owed me something. After a few weeks of diligent searching, I broached the subject of early retirement with my spouse. I pointed out that due to my medical issues, it was unlikely that anyone would hire me. Sherri was having none of it, though. While I unofficially eased into early retirement, my spouse reminded me that "you're not retired, buddy, you're unemployed." For several months I collected unemployment and ate up much of our savings.

To appease my slave-driving spouse, despite considering myself retired, I continued job hunting. I was interviewing in a nearby town for an opportunity that combined insurance and investments in an entrepreneurial venture that, only a few years earlier, I would have considered extremely appealing. Now though, I was beginning to sense that my mission in life was about more than helping would-be clients build their retirement plans.

During the biographical paperwork portion of the interview, I got a text detailing the demise of my former RIO (Radar Intercept Officer). Lulu had been a law professor in Ohio and had recently lost his battle with cancer. The last time I'd seen him was at a minor league (Durham Bulls) baseball game in Tidewater, Virginia, in 2003. Lulu, Sweat, and I had met there for a mini-reunion of sorts.

I found myself staring at a blank biographical questionnaire, tears streaming down my cheeks. The gentleman interviewing me noticed. I ended up explaining the situation. To his credit, he must have overlooked it because the company did end up offering the opportunity to continue in the interview process. By then, though, I had moved on.

Sweat and I had intended to visit Lulu and, for the last few months, had been working through the logistics of making it happen. Alas, for various reasons, that visit never materialized.

Just a couple of days before Lulu's memorial, I took a job selling supplemental medical insurance as an independent agent working for a company whose mascot is a duck.

I spent time studying for my Health Insurance License and took the test the day before flying out to Lulu's memorial service. I failed. My heart was not in it. I went out to Virginia, where the smartest guy I've ever known was laid to rest. Of course, smart isn't necessarily good. Lulu was also a good man.

Back in Iowa, some days later, I retook the Health Insurance Exam. This time I passed.

The position was guaranteed to make us successful and prosperous. Assuming I could stick it out. Building a book of business sufficient to support us would take time. "Time is money," and in a nutshell, the financial bridge we would be forced to cross (read: reach breakeven) was a span that turned out longer than our savings could support. So, after ninety days and six thousand miles on my vehicle, during which I had grossed about fifteen hundred dollars, it became painfully obvious that although long-term success was possible, nay even likely, getting from here to there was a "bridge too far."

So, there we were, retired again or unemployed, depending on whose perspective you choose to embrace. All the while, our savings, once—if not substantial, at least adequate—continued to dwindle.

In those days, my military pension was less than twenty thousand a year, not nearly enough to live on. My plan shifted to increasing my disability rating and thus my pension, so I could afford to retire.

With more time on my hands, I continued my job search but, more importantly, began a deeper dive into my faith. I continued as a witness at CRHP retreats. After a long phase of passive membership, I started attending Knights of Columbus[51] meetings. As the potential for new members for future CRHP retreats began to dwindle, the parish decided to suspend them indefinitely. After eight weekend retreats, seven of them attended by "yours truly," I would attempt to fill the impending void by increased involvement with the Knights of Columbus. After six months of attending meetings, I took the next steps, becoming a second and then third-degree Knight. Then in the spring of 2016, one year after becoming active once again, I became a fourth-degree Knight.

As I became more serious about my faith, others noticed the change in me. Sherri perceived it as well and, with some added gentle persuasion from friends, attended a women's CRHP retreat. Moreover, the person who hates public speaking more than anyone I know signed up as a presenter for the next. Our most important job as husbands and fathers is to get our

---

[51] The Knights of Columbus is the world's largest lay Catholic organization, with more than 1.8 million members around the world. The order was founded 130 years ago in 1882 by Venerable Father Michael J. McGivney at St. Mary's Church in New Haven, Connecticut. The original intent to provide welfare and security for families during times of sickness and death has grown so that last year, Knights donated more than 70 million hours of volunteer time and $158 million to charity. The order is currently headed by Supreme Knight Patrick E. Kelly.

wives and children to Heaven. It's something I think about a lot.

Chapter Twenty-One:
Battle Stations

"Ancient Christians called on the Blessed Mother with the title Stella Maris, or Star of the Sea, because they saw her as a guiding light for wayward 'mariners' navigating the stormy waters of life."[52] Despite not having been at sea for many years, the deeper I dug into my faith, the more I realized that I was still a "wayward mariner" of sorts.

I'd also been awakened to the fact that there had been a "war" right in front of me all along. In his *Apostolic Exhortation to Catholic Men*, entitled *Into the Breach*, Bishop Thomas J. Olmstead implores us,

[52] Our Lady, Star of the Sea is an ancient title for the Virgin Mary. The words Star of the Sea are a translation of the Latin Stella Maris. The title has been in use since at least the early medieval period. Originally arising from a scribal error in a supposed etymology of the name Mary, it came to be seen as allegorical of Mary's role as "guiding star" on the way to Christ. Under this name, the Virgin Mary is believed to intercede as a guide and protector of seafarers in particular. The Apostleship of the Sea, and many coastal churches are named Stella Maris or Star of the Sea. - Mirjana Soldo, "My Heart Will Triumph," pg. 337

saying, "Men, do not hesitate to engage in the battle that is raging all around you."

"And I sought for a man among them who should build up the wall and stand in the breach before me and the land..." Ezekiel 22:30

All along, God had been leading me to this moment. I got to say, it seems like a somewhat circuitous route; and if you've made it this far, I'm sure you'll agree. That said, a more direct route would have gotten me here prematurely. No doubt I would not have been prepared to listen, to follow. Last year I wrote a prayer about it:

Patient Teacher, Gentle Friend
Jesus, I know You are my personal savior
My whole life, You waited for me
I spent most of it in darkness
I've harmed many, including myself, through arrogance and ignorance.
Yet through the decades, You waited patiently
In Your time, I've come to see the light
I understand that You were my friend all along,
even when I didn't know it myself
I've finally learned that the most important thing all along
Was simply to know You.
Help me know You better, to listen
and to become half the friend You have always been to me

"Deep in his heart, every man longs for a battle to fight, an adventure to live, and a beauty to rescue."[53] Ultimately, that's an apt description of why I, and many others, answer our nation's call to serve. As a Navy fighter pilot, legitimate battle alluded me, but I did manage enough adventure to last a few lifetimes. I'm not sure I rescued a beauty either. If anything, the beauty in my life rescued me. Yet all my battles and adventures are not relegated to the dustbin of history. God, in His infinite wisdom, has placed new ones squarely in front of me.

I'm not sure how it will all unfold. I only know that the first half of my life was all about me and mine. Okay, mostly me. Yet, God had a different plan all along. Who knew? My life is so different from the one I imagined. I imagined some pretty great things. My backup plan was United or Delta or FedEx, and in my spare time, I would write books and/or renew my stockbroker's license. On the other hand, if things went particularly well, at some point, I would retire from the military, run for political office, win, and the rest would be history that someday students would be compelled to learn.

I shake my head when I think about what a fool I was. "True strength does not come out of bravado. Until we are broken, our life will be self-centered, self-reliant; our strength will be our own. So long as you think you are really something in and of yourself, what will you need God for?"[54]

I think of Lazarus, who Jesus raised from the dead. I think of how his sister Martha went out to meet Jesus

---

[53] John Eldredge, "Wild at Heart: Discovering the Secret of a Man's Soul"

[54] Ibid

and, depending on how you interpret her words, either accusatory or faith-filled, said to Jesus, *"Lord, if you had been here, my brother would not have died."* John 11:21

Those familiar with the story know that Jesus purposefully delayed his arrival.

"So, when he heard that he was ill, he remained for two days in the place where he was." John 11:6

In our stupor of human ignorance, we think God will do something miraculous in accordance with our dreams or wishes. Martha was certain Jesus could have cured Lazarus of whatever ultimately killed him. But Jesus had bigger plans for Lazarus that far exceeded the hopes of any mortal being, before or since.

I, too, had a dream. I envisioned a future perfectly sublime, but now I know it was small compared to what God has in store for me. Now I am on a path not of my own choosing, and it is wonderful.

"For a moment, wasn't I a king, but if I'd only known how the king would fall, hey, who's to say? You know I might have changed it all."[55] My fall was not quite done just yet. Truth be told, I'm still falling (read: failing). A part of me cares. Truly I do. Mostly, though, I don't worry about my job. My friend Eric from my second and third CRHP was always fond of saying, "my job is what I do. It's not who I am."

Sadly, many men and women in this nation—I used to be their chief, by the way—identify themselves according to their occupation. Of course, my professional demise, my race to oblivion, was a tough pill to swallow. Multiple Sclerosis, its impact on my

55 "The Dance," by Tony Arata, performed by Garth Brooks

cognitive abilities—none too extraordinary to begin with—has driven me to this place, originally as black as any dark night in the Indian Ocean. Yet today, I have been led from that darkness and into the light. I am as happy as I've ever been. Happy isn't even the right word. Content doesn't capture it either. It's all that and more. Like the Yuletide song says, maybe it's "comfort and joy?" I'm not rich, and I'm not famous. I'm not held in particularly high esteem by my fellow man. No one could or should ever mistake me for our nation's thirty-fifth president. Yet, I am at peace. I can't explain it except to say that my peace flows like a river from our Lord.

"If there is meaning to our suffering, we can go through anything, but if there is no meaning, we will slip into despair."[56] Quite simply, the purpose of my suffering—I feel kind of funny even calling it that, after all, I'm not in any pain or anything, I'm just a little unsteady on my feet and don't think as fast as I used to—is twofold. First, it has changed the way I think. I no longer do only that which satisfies "my will." Today before I act, I think to myself, "Does what I'm about to do advance the will of God?" More accurately, I strive to fulfill God's will first. In so doing, I'm also doing a better job as "my brother's keeper."

"And now, bless the God of all,
who has done wondrous things on earth:
Who fosters people's growth from their mother's womb,
and fashions them according to His will!
May He grant you joy of heart

---

[56] Pope St. John Paul II, Salvifici Doloris

and may peace abide among you:
May His goodness toward us endure in Israel
to deliver us in our days." Sir 50:22-24

Alas, I must report this is a tall order and one where I often fail. How do I know God's will? In a word, prayer. Once again, this is an "Achilles Heel" for me. My failings, most of them improving, still plague me because I don't pray enough. A prime example is this little missive you are reading. Instead of telling you about my conversion story, I could be praying. The question one must ask is this tale itself a sin? I wonder about this; pray about it, yet I find that I am compelled to continue. Is my mission delusional?

Before the introspection of such navel gazing consumes me, allow me to continue. In 2015, during my fourth or fifth CRHP, my friend Paul offered to take me out on his tandem bicycle. The guy is a serious biker. I think he has a bike for every day of the week. In Iowa, there is this big annual bike event called RAGBRAI.[57] Paul does it every year. He rides a bike to work nearly every day as well.

He had purchased the tandem years earlier in an optimistic though ultimately misguided attempt to get his bride to ride. My first ride was indescribably liberating. I was cruising along through God's wondrous bounty, enjoying the sights and sounds and the aromas of wildflowers that grow along the bike trail. My first ride with Paul and my CRHP brothers Shannon and Wade—

[57] RAGBRAI is an acronym and registered trademark for the Register's Annual Great Bicycle Ride Across Iowa, which is a non-competitive bicycle ride organized by The Des Moines Register, which goes across the U.S. state of Iowa from west to east, that draws recreational riders from across the United States and many foreign countries. First held in 1973, RAGBRAI is the largest bike-touring event in the world.

all three fellow Knights—was indeed an adventure. I used to love the outdoors, hunting, fishing, camping, or simply going for a run. Riding on the back of Paul's tandem has become a regular thing for me now. We've done the annual MS Bike Ride a couple of times. I've joined him for a day of RAGBRAI twice. On that first ride, we just went to a neighboring town for a beer. I think it was a total roundtrip of only 25 miles, but my ass was sore for a week.

Riding a tandem bike is perfect because it allows a guy with a compromised equilibrium to feel the wind in his hair and get a workout that I once thought was no longer possible. However, that's not what's truly miraculous. What's significant with Paul and the cast of friends who ride with us is that they're all graduates of multiple CRHP (Christ Renews His Parish) weekends. All are members of the Knights of Columbus. They are faith-filled men, each in their way "filling the breach,"[58] and in so doing, they serve as fine examples for others they encounter. They are not only companions on the bicycle paths of Central Iowa, but they are also my companions, guides, really, on my journey toward eternal life.

Wade is fond of reminding anyone and everyone that "God is good, all the time, all the time, God is good." And my personal favorite, "If Christianity were a crime, would there be enough evidence to convict you?" Wade and his entire family are living examples for others they encounter. For years he's ministered at the nearest prison. That's only one of the ways he's the hands and feet of Jesus here on earth.

Shannon was the Grand Knight of our council when I got re-energized and became active in the Knights of Columbus. He had gone to my high school, so I knew

[58] "Into the Breach," Bishop Thomas J. Olmstead, Phoenix Diocese.

him, but he became my true friend when he and I attended our Parish's first CRHP. He's funny and more than a bit mischievous, but he's also extremely conscientious and kind and smart. I consider myself fortunate to call him friend. He's the one who first suggested the title of this book.

Paul is the man who first offered a bike ride. His entire life is—and as far as I can tell, has always been—a testament, an example for the rest of us on the road to eternal bliss. While the rest of us try to stay on the straight and narrow path, Paul is up ahead, gesturing for us to follow. He's like a scoutmaster or infantry soldier, but this isn't a nature walk or even taking a hill on some war-torn landscape. No, this battle is for our souls.

Saint Augustine once wrote that "Friendship is the elixir of life." I'd be remiss if I didn't mention a few of my CRHP and/or Knights of Columbus brothers. Paul, and Paul, and Joe, and Joe, and Joe, and Steve, and Steve, and Steve, and Dave, and Dave, and Dave, and Dan, and Dan, and Dan, and Tony, and Ken, and Ken, and Kenny, and John, and Jodi, and Bret, and Larry, and Larry, and Larry, and Marty, and Dale, and Fred, and Fred, and Travis, and Dcn. Tom, and Tom, and Scott, and Scott and Phil, and Shannon and Wade, and Merlyn, and Jamie, and Doug, and Marc, and Mark, and Chris, and Ed, and Craig, and Brian, and Eric, and Dcn. Dennis, Fr. Dominic, and so many other Christian men who have become my comrades in the battle raging all around us.

"I don't trust a man who hasn't suffered; I don't let a man get close to me who hasn't faced his wound. Think of the posers you know—are they the kind of man you would call at 2:00 A.M. when life is collapsing around you?" Not me. I don't want clichés; I want deep, soulful truth, and that only comes when a man has walked the road I've been talking about."[59]

It has taken me more than half of a century to learn this simple lesson. I've been so very fortunate in my lifetime to know the right people, all true friends, at precisely the right time. "Every man carries a wound. I have never met a man without one. No matter how good your life may have seemed to you, you live in a broken world full of broken people."[60]

During this time, let's call it a revelation of sorts, I came to the realization that helping others will naturally minimize the significance of my own plight. My own "relatively tiny" cross seems lighter when I do something for my fellow man. Who knew? Apparently, everyone. "No one is useless in this world who lightens the burdens of another."—Charles Dickens

That said, sometimes, I still need help. At those times, I try to think of Jesus. Have you ever considered Jesus's march to Golgotha or how Simon of Cyrene[61] was pressed into service to help him bear his cross? This

---

[59] John Eldredge, "Wild at Heart Revised and Updated: Discovering the Secret of a Man's Soul"

[60] Ibid

[61] Simon of Cyrene is mentioned in Matthew, Mark and Luke. Matthew only records his name and place of origin (27:32), but Mark and Luke say that he was "on his way in from the country" (Luke 23:26). Mark provides the most information about Simon, adding that he was "the father of Alexander and Rufus" (Mark 15:21)

was a simple yet profound lesson from Jesus for all eternity. Jesus, a.k.a. God, did not need help to get his cross to Calvary. He could have simply commanded a legion of Angels to fly it up there. The simple yet profound lesson is that sometimes your cross might get too heavy to bear, and it's okay to let others help you. It's grace, both given and received.

Do you Believe? If asked, most of us believe in God. I don't recall a time in my life when I couldn't recite the Nicene Creed. Yet, for most of us, our answer isn't really an answer. It's more an intellectual exercise that allows for the possibility that a supreme being does, in fact, exist. I do not remember a time when I didn't believe, but it's only recently, after over half a century, that the words in the Creed have gained purchase. Today I know in my heart that God exists. I truly believe it.

In my original memoir, *The Gift*, I made much of the adjustment to my new life. Dreams die slowly, painfully. Yet, the death of one dream has left ample space for something more precious than gold. It all seems so sudden. As I look back, though, despite the challenge I received from my friend Joe on the first night of my very first CRHP, the changes in my life have been gradual, gentle, and joyful. I ask myself how, why me? I suppose the health issues that I have endured have caused me to consider my own mortality. If you want to do better in your life, think about your death.

What do you want to be remembered for? I've thought about this a lot. My entire life has been a series of desperate attempts to achieve immortality. Foolishly, I wanted to write because I wanted to be remembered. I wanted some record of the fact that I'd been here.

A Different Kind of War

It's taken me more than half a century to figure this out, but today when asked what I'd like to be remembered for, my answer is nothing. By conventional human standards, that sounds rather apathetic. Yet, I no longer strive for success here on earth. Instead, I strive for Heaven.

"He must increase: I must decrease." John the Baptist, Jn 3:30

Chapter Twenty-Two:

The Captain of My Soul

By the end of 2015, I was once again retired after my brief foray into Insurance Sales, but once again, Sherri saw it differently. Now, though, instead of scouring the countryside for opportunities, I hunted primarily through electronic means, job boards, and such. This left me ample time to enjoy my sabbatical. Enjoy it, I did, with old friends and new ones. I began to recognize a change in me so gradual that it was barely noticeable. I was kinder, slightly more empathetic, and it sounds ridiculous when I say it, so ask my friends, humbler. I guess there's still enough fighter pilot in me to brag about my humility.

When I wrote my novella-sized memoir, *The Gift*, over a decade ago, little snippets of my future were foreshadowed. I know how this happened, but for those of you who aren't buying what I'm selling, no explanation will suffice. For those of you who already believe, none is necessary.

Anyhow, "I think of one's destiny as the channel stretching out before us on life's journey; within that channel, we have the freedom to shape our path."[62] Yes, I wrote that last bit in 2006. My logic has evolved some. In the main, I still believe that our destiny, aka the will of God, is largely predetermined. Fight it, or go with the flow, but you're going downstream. Yet, within the channel itself, one has the freedom to navigate as one sees fit, a.k.a. free will.

So, while William Ernest Henley's poem "Invictus" is truly inspirational, at least for the first half of my life. For the latter half, it's largely "road apples."[63]

Invictus

"Out of the night that covers me,
Black as the pit from pole to pole,
I thank whatever gods may be
For my unconquerable soul.

In the fell clutch of circumstance
I have not winced nor cried aloud.
Under the bludgeonings of chance
My head is bloody, but unbowed.

Beyond this place of wrath and tears
Looms but the Horror of the shade,
And yet the menace of the years
Finds and shall find me unafraid.

It matters not how strait the gate,
How charged with punishments the scroll,
I am the master of my fate,
I am the captain of my soul."

Today I know that I am not really the "Master of my fate," though I should strive to be at least a co-captain of my soul. Instead, I prefer the philosophy of Garth,

[62] Kendall Geneser, "The Gift," pg. 121-122

[63] Road Apples is a common euphemism for horse shit.

"but with the good Lord as my Captain, I can make it through them all."[64]

In the summer of 2016, I became the Grand Knight of our local Knights of Columbus Council. Joe had first encouraged me, asking if I'd be willing to accept nomination as our Deputy Grand Knight. That normally should have lasted for two years, but my good friend Travis, then the Grand Knight, decided that he needed to step down after a year as career demands were impeding his ability to do justice to the post. By the way, it's a bold and courageous thing to admit that something is too much, especially for the overall good of the organization. Travis and his wife had also decided they wanted to start their family. Today they have a beautiful young son, Isiah. They also recently added their daughter, Mikah.

So, I gradually found myself ensconced in the religion that I'd always taken for granted. The more I learned, the more beautiful I found the Church to be. To be sure, there are many things desperately wrong with the Catholic Church. One must simply listen to the news. Yet, if you were charged with destroying Christianity—as the Devil most certainly is—might your focus not be on the Church that was founded by Jesus himself? Archbishop Fulton Sheen once said, "There are not one hundred people in the United States who hate the Catholic Church, but there are millions who hate what they wrongly perceive the Catholic Church to be."

As my personal "skin in the game" continued to grow, as I continued to open that "next door," a rather insidious thing happened. I developed a sense of

64 Garth Brooks, "Sail My Vessel"

mission. I decided that despite my ever-increasing physical and mental limitations, I would indulge in this newfound mission.

"To know your mission and not to follow it is one of the greatest human miseries."[65] I've always had a sense of mission; from age seven to twenty-one, it was baseball. From age twenty-two to age thirty-four, it was flying Navy jets. From age thirty-four to age fifty-one, it was becoming some sort of success (as measured by society). Originally, my mission was all about me and my will. Now, late in the third, but most likely early in the fourth quarter of life, my mission is based on the will of Him who made me.

My most glaring failure is as a father. While I chased my own dreams and then later licked my wounds (post-diagnosis), my kids grew up in what was essentially a broken home. Oh, there wasn't anything untoward, no domestic violence or anything. I wouldn't even characterize it as neglect. I think my boys know I love them and am proud of the men they've become despite my lackluster parental guidance. While my child-rearing technique was not out and out neglect, per se, I guess I would call it indifference. That, as any decent father would tell you, is no way to raise children.

The past is the past, and we can't get it back. We can only do better with the time we have left. When I was young and cocksure, arrogance told me that my mission in life was destined to be of some historical significance. I looked beyond the most important missions right in front of me, namely my family. In athletics, coaches will often tell players to "stay within

---

65 Matthew Kelly, "Perfectly Yourself, pg. 175

yourself," as players will sometimes try to do too much—be more than the role they are meant to fulfill for their respective team. Unfortunately, most of the first half of my life was spent with me looking well beyond my role, beyond my actual mission. Sadly, while I gazed at the distant horizon of my dreams, life happened. Then while I peered at my navel, feeling sorry for myself, time kept marching on. When I finally looked up, my kids were grown. It has taken me more than half a century to sluice out what my mission was from the beginning.

In 2017, I began working in a call center for a large insurance firm. The company is a third-party administrator of benefits for companies primarily in North America. The training was very thorough, and I soon had both my Life and Health Insurance License in all fifty states.

My official title was Benefits Counselor. I was working for the first time in my life as an hourly employee. For those of you keeping score at home, this was an example of my continued toboggan ride toward oblivion. In accord with my historical career progression, I was working harder for less money. That said, helping people from all over our country to make sense of their company's healthcare was a continually rewarding experience.

Despite helping customers, I was never fast enough. Management was soon leaning on me to continue my helpful ways but to do it faster. However, attempts to speed up resulted in an increased error rate. Due to my somewhat compromised motor skills, coupled with cognitive issues, speeding up caused mistakes. I started attracting unwanted attention because I had hit a wall with respect to my performance which tended to be below average. My direct managers were patient, but I was eventually offered another (less demanding) position. And so, my toboggan ride continues. My new gig is less intellectually demanding and much lower pressure. Yet my performance is still suspect. If I were asked to read the writing plainly scrawled on the wall, my working life is nearing its somewhat discreditable conclusion. Though I would not mind a few more years of working, I am not afraid.

Our final fish fry for the Lenten Season happened a few nights ago. Our little chapter runs arguably the best fish fry in central Iowa. We're also one of the last groups that charge a "free will" donation for an all-you-can-eat experience. The result is that Lent, besides being a time of prayer, fasting, and abstinence, is also the time that Knights of Columbus across America—but certainly in our little chapter—do the bulk of their fundraising. For six weeks in the spring, we're working diligently to give our customers a fine dining experience. We offer great food and great fellowship to people from all over the community and beyond. If it sounds like I'm bragging, I am. The Council I belong to has about one hundred and sixty (give or take), but a cadre of about twenty-five men make the magic happen. Along with our local Catholic Women's Club (who make our delicious desserts) as well as student volunteers, in two hours, we feed about six hundred guests. We then spend most of the rest of the year spending that money on worthy charitable causes.

By the time we come to our next Lent, we're usually down to less than a thousand dollars in our coffers. By then, we've given several thousand dollars away to the homeless, the abused, prisoners, students, Special

Olympics, and a myriad of other worthy causes. So yes, I guess I am bragging just a little. On behalf of the Knights of Columbus and potential Knights everywhere, doing good feels good. Despite one's own issues, helping our fellow humans makes you feel all warm and fuzzy inside. I suppose I would describe it as utter peace and contentment. I suspect it is why right now I'm the happiest I have ever been in my life, and that includes our "salad days," that magical time spent as a Desert Bogey. I'm proud to be associated with such a fine cadre of Christian men.

"Do not boast about tomorrow for you do not know what a day may bring." Proverbs 27:1

On August 21st, 2017, the day of a solar eclipse, I saw a headline asking "if the eclipse was evidence of God's existence," to which I would say, gee, ya think? I suppose that it is only a strange coincidence that the sun is roughly four hundred times larger than the moon but is also four hundred times farther away from Earth, thus rendering them—from our earthly vantage point—the same size. This optical sleight of hand is what makes a total eclipse possible. In all the universe, the odds of such an amazing coincidence are truly astounding. While coincidence is plausible, it's not likely, and thus implies that an intelligent design exists.

In my opinion, it takes a bigger leap of faith to know this, as most scientists do, and still be an atheist or agnostic, as many scientists profess. That's only one example, though. There are many examples in many scientific disciplines as miraculous as any solar eclipse. I used to believe in things like luck and coincidence. Now I'm certain that things I once chalked up to chance are often the result of God's grand design. My friend and CRHP sister, a fellow parishioner, Mary Ann, put it this way in a bible study class we were attending: "Non-believers only believe what they can see, while Christians often see what they believe."

In September of 2017, I reunited with some of my old Navy buds at what I now refer to as the first annual "Sleepy Hollow Reunion" because it was largely comprised of Pilots and RIOs who had once resided forward on the O2 level of CV-62, USS Independence - affectionately known as "Sleepy Hollow." We met at Slim's house in Atlanta, Georgia. We were there for three days and had the best time. On the next to last day there, my friend "Naked" met us for tennis. Pilots vs. Rios. I watched but cheered for the "single anchor team."[66] Naked and I had been Bogey drivers together in the high desert. He had been at the Naval Academy and was originally a west coast Tomcat guy. Point being, though he had never lived in "Sleepy Hollow," he is well known by all of us and well-liked. He is most certainly considered an inaugural member of our intimate but growing group.

Naked was late showing up for tennis, explaining that he had come directly from a CRHP meeting. He said it so matter-of-factly, so nonchalantly, that it took my breath away. Here was a man's man, not particularly trying, as men so often do in America, to hide his faith. By simply mentioning his previous engagement, he was opening the door in a quiet, understated way to

66 Naval Aviators, (i.e. Pilot Wings feature a single anchor], while Naval Flight Officer (i.e., RIO [Radar Intercept Officer] Wings have two smaller ones).

evangelize his brothers. When I say that, I am not suggesting that Naked even knew or thought of this as evangelization, but if anyone knew, truly knew what he had so casually placed at our respective doorsteps, someone surely would have asked him about it. No one did. No one said, 'CRHP, what's that?' The one other guy in the room that understood the great door that had opened just a crack remained silent. I never said a word about it. The opportunity passed as the conversation turned. I sipped my beer and marveled at my lack of intestinal fortitude.

> "Much will be required of the person entrusted with much, and still more will be demanded of the person entrusted with more."—Jesus, Gospel of Luke 12:48

How do you know for sure that Michelangelo painted the ceiling of the Sistine Chapel? Or that Leonardo da Vinci was responsible for the Mona Lisa? Were you there? Of course not. Your understanding of reality and truth is dependent on the documented testimony of credible witnesses. Yet when we weigh the credibility of huge events in history, many discount the possibility that Jesus was, in fact, God incarnate and that he rose from the dead.

We take for granted that Colonel Chamberlain held the flank of the Union army on Little Roundtop or that General Washington crossed the Delaware. Why? Because there were numerous credible witnesses reporting on these events. Yet, not one of the witnesses was questioned on pain of death to test their resolve.

In contrast, eleven of twelve apostles were martyred—mostly by the Romans in their misguided attempt to get them to recant their stories. Bartholomew was skinned alive. During the process of being flayed, he never changed his story. That is as strong a reason for faith as I can fathom. If your faith needs a little reason—as mine sometimes does—the fact that not one of them changed their story is prima facie evidence. If the whole resurrection deal is a lie, if I am Bartholomew, after the first slice of my own flesh, I would have been screaming at the top of my lungs, "JUST KIDDING! WE STOLE THE BODY!" He never changed his story. Instead, he prayed for those torturing him to death.

My life is so different from the one I had envisioned. I grew up in a hyper-secular household, not because both of my parents were not knowledgeable Christians, but because they were. Mom was Lutheran, and Dad was Catholic. Mom was a smart lady and somewhat militant in her distaste for Papists. Dad was raised, immersed really, in the infallible authority of the Holy Roman See. Dad, and indeed most, were insufficiently armed to combat my mother's logical blitzkrieg. To preserve the peace, dad seldom challenged my mother on her ideas concerning Catholicism. To preserve the peace, a compromise was reached. My sister and I were raised Catholic, but we were educated in public schools. Church on Sunday was obligatory, but we were last in, first out kind of attendees. Ideas like transubstantiation of the eucharist, reconciliation, or Mary's immaculate conception were, in mom's eyes, silly superstition. "Not only was Mary the mother of Him who is born [in Bethlehem], but of Him who, before the world, was eternally born of the Father." —Martin Luther, on the divine motherhood of Mary.

My mother had grown up in a world where Catholics were a bunch of statue-worshiping fish eaters who could go out and drink you under the table on Friday, confess their sins on Saturday and then look down their noses at the lesser denominations the rest of the week.

One thing I did learn early is that there are many valid paths to our personal sanctification, and all paths don't go through the Holy Catholic and Apostolic Church. Some of the most righteous people I know aren't Catholic. A few of them aren't even Christian. I was proud to understand the difference between catholic and Catholic at an early age; the whole little "c" versus big "C" thing.

Yet, despite my mother's dismissal of some Catholic practices and beliefs, despite the seemingly justified logic of her assertions—at least in my own Lilliputian cranial structure—later in life, after my own renewal, I would begin an exhaustive investigation of my faith. This investigation will no doubt last for the rest of my earthly life. What I've found so far is that my mom, God love her, was wrong. The more I learn, the more I marvel at the beauty of the church. Archbishop Sheen was right. People don't hate Catholicism. They simply hate what they mistakenly think Catholicism is.

Catholicism embodies every means of sanctification, things like scripture, tradition, the sacraments, and the magisterium. In other words, the church holds every key to achieving wisdom and, ultimately, eternal salvation. Why then isn't every Christian a Catholic? Fr. John Riccardo says it best, if I may paraphrase, the reason more people aren't beating down the doors to become Catholic is mostly because of Catholics. I believe his point is that we Catholics must strive to do a better job welcoming our brothers and sisters from other faith traditions and that we must try to exhibit a better example for all those we encounter.

Having said that, it is not at all the same world my parents grew up in. Today it is not Catholics vs. Protestants. It's Christians vs. agnostics/atheists—the so-called "nones." My Protestant brothers and sisters are my teammates in the battle against moral relativism, where a post-Christian world looks on people like us as though we're bigoted, flat-earthers, primitive, naive, and stupid. As a fellow glass-house dweller—after all, I've managed to raise two agnostics—I must point out that "vs." isn't the exact term here. I know that conversion cannot be forced. It must happen by example, gently, over time, and with love.

"Come to Me, all you who labor and are burdened, and I will give you rest. Take My yoke upon you and learn from Me, for I am meek and humble of heart; and you will find rest for yourselves. For My yoke is easy, and My burden light."—Jesus, Gospel of Matthew 11:28-30

All I know is that I'm trying to set that example. I pray that I'm not too late. Now I'm on a path not of my own choosing, and it is wonderful.

The Path of Righteousness

Lord, let me always do Your will
Grant me the vision to see the right path
And the wisdom to choose it
Grant me courage along the way
And strength to finish the journey

Give me faith to share with my companions
And at journeys end an eternity with You.

Chapter Twenty-Three:

Comenasai

Originally, I had assumed that the focus of my mission would be associated with the laudable goal of combating Multiple Sclerosis. In fact, for many years, I volunteered as the coordinator of a small men's group in central Iowa. Sponsored by the National Multiple Sclerosis Society (NMSS), the focus of our mission was simply to do some fun "guy" stuff a few times a year for guys with limited mobility. We went fishing, did some faux gaming in the poker room of a local casino, and attended a baseball game and a winery. In fact, the proceeds of my first attempt to tell this story, *The Gift*, were used to help fund those efforts. Yet, as I became more ensconced in my growing faith, I found myself becoming less and less involved in NMSS projects/initiatives. I eventually relinquished my duties.

The genesis of my transformation is ongoing, and while chronicling my metamorphosis was meant to be inspirational, the effort harbors a dark undertone that needed my immediate attention.

I've tried to wax eloquent about how a seemingly terrible thing, MS, has ultimately saved me and how my spiritual awakening continues to this day. Yet my good friend Joe, after reading a rough draft, said he found the work "disturbing."

For those in need of a quick refresher, it was his initial "shot across the bow" that got me thinking about how I was living my life (see chapter 19), saying, "Well, Kendall, I've been a Knight for six years. How come I've never seen you at a meeting?"

We usually recognize the elephant lurking in the opposite corner of the room. Sometimes, though, we need a friend to make the introduction. Joe is not bashful about sharing his opinion. It is one of the things I love about the guy. A real friend will keep you honest, he makes me assess and reassess my life frequently, and I try to do the same for him.

The crux of the issue boils down to two words, selfish pride. In nearly every conceivable way, I have, until very recently, managed to supplant the needs of others to fulfill my own. As such, the things I revered were given precedence over those of my loved ones.

Joe pointed out the error of my ways one morning over coffee. He asked a simple question. "Why do you grow a beard in the winter?"

"I like not having to shave. It keeps my face warm," I said.

"Is that all?"

"I like how it looks, I guess."

"How's Sherri like it?"

"She hates it," I said. "She was complaining about it this morning. I told her I'd be shaving it off soon. She doesn't like to kiss me."

"How do you think it feels for her?" he asked.

I shrugged.

"When I can, I like to do nice things for my wife," he said. "I try to do things I think she might like. Little things."

Just like that, he showed me the error in my logic.

The beard is but an example, a final vestige, if you will, of a stunning lack of compassion, a blind spot that envelops my whole family. While this work has hopefully highlighted the positive changes in my life, there is still plenty of room for improvement.

My selfishness has taken many forms over many years. During my time as a fighter pilot, it was akin to addiction and, in retrospect—like some sort of shape-shifting apparition—all my domestic relationships have suffered on account of the addiction du jour.

When I flew, my addiction was overt. When I was striving to become a mover and shaker in the world of finance, my addiction, though less pronounced, was still there. It resulted in a master's degree in business but, alas, also two young men—my boys—adrift in a confusing world. All because during their formative years, their father was mostly MIA.

Yet the dark undertones of this work that Joe was kind enough to point out—although I'd always recognized them—mainly concern the damage I've done in my marriage. The idea that MS is partly to blame is a decent excuse, but an excuse, nonetheless. After all, I am the guy that once said, "Hi, honey. Show me where I live."

I am on a path that will hopefully make the world around me a better place and, with God's kindness, as St. Paul said, "lead to my repentance." Yet, if you have made it this far, you know for certain that my long-suffering wife deserves every kindness and consideration that her less-than-stellar life partner (me) can offer.

As a result, I now know that—much like those addicted to drugs or alcohol—I must make amends.

Step nine in the AA handbook is to make direct amends to such people wherever possible, except when to do so would injure them or others. Although I have never been addicted to drugs or alcohol, addictions of various sorts have plagued me and rendered harm to those closest to me. It is my intent to make amends with my immediate family members. I do not know if the damage I've done makes successful contrition possible.

I tried with my oldest son first. I felt sort of sick to my stomach and the effort—though I'm sure he didn't notice—made my knees as shaky as a moonless night trap.

"Nick, I have something I need to discuss with you." He stood in front of the fridge, contemplating a late-night snack.

"It's kind of hard to talk about. It's actually gonna suck... for me anyway."

"What is it?" he said impatiently.

"I need to make amends."

"What? What for?"

I decided to rip the band-aid off and plunge headlong into it. "I wasn't a good Dad. After MS, I sort of laid down on the job. I feel like in many ways I wasn't there for you."

"I never felt that way," he said. "I'm still here," he added and beat a hasty retreat toward his room, snack in hand.

I went back to my chair, both elated and deflated. I'd left so much unsaid. Yet I was relieved that, to some degree, he'd let me off the hook. Then, halfway up the stairs, he added, "I've never felt that way, Dad. Never."

My God. Such mercy. Such wisdom. Though I understand and accept the error of my ways, my son either does not perceive or does not take account of my failures.

"You have anointed my head with oil:
My cup overflows."—Psalm 23 / (part of verse 5)

I next wanted to visit with my youngest son. Unlike my oldest—who still lives at home -making a connection, from a logistical standpoint, is not so simple.

One evening I broached the subject with Sherri.

"I just told him that after my diagnosis, I wasn't the Dad I should've been, and, as a result, he and his brother sort of got screwed," I added.

"Why?" she asked.

"Well, I feel like most of my life, I've been selfish. For a lot of their childhood, I've put my own needs above those of my kids."

Sherri was uncharacteristically silent. I can only imagine the thoughts racing through her head. Today I wonder if years of inattention had irreversibly damaged the most important relationship of my life.

"All men make mistakes, but a good man yields when he knows his course is wrong and repairs the evil. The only sin is pride." - Sophocles

Next, I attempted to broach the subject with my youngest. Finding an opportunity for a one-on-one discussion proved difficult. I met him at his home one spring afternoon. Both he and his brother are capable handymen, and he was in the throes of a plumbing project at his home. We conversed about his project, and I marveled at his ability to do things—things he had never learned from his father.

"How'd you figure all this stuff out?" I said.

"Trial and error," he answered "...and YouTube," he added.

"Well, I was here to get you to sign a card for your mom, but truth be told, I'm also here to ask you what you thought about growing up."

He looked at me kind of strangely, but I continued. "You know I'm nearly finished with the expanded version of my memoir." I wanted to include something about my parenting skills, or lack thereof. "See, I feel like you got short-changed growing up. I mean, I did so much with your older brother, and then, when I was starting to shift my focus toward you, that is when I got MS. So, I feel as though you got a raw deal. Like I let you down as a father. I didn't do near as much with you, and for that, I'm sorry." Like his older brother, my youngest son let me off easy, saying, "Yeah, I never felt neglected or anything. You're a good dad."

He took a break to let the spray foam that he had applied dry. He showed me some of the "how-to" video clips that he had accumulated while we visited, and that was it. Like his big brother, I marveled at the grace the young man displayed and extended. Though I often lament the fact that my boys are basically agnostic in the practice of their faith—and I pray daily for their eventual reversion and/or reconciliation—their example of forgiveness and love are two of the most Christian things that I have ever seen.

I stayed for a few minutes longer, but I could see that my son was anxious to finish his plumbing project, and Sherri and I were going to church later that afternoon, so I left. Yet, that wasn't the end of it. That evening, hours after our visit, my son sent me a text. Obviously, he'd given his response some more thought. This is what he said:

'So, I might have lied earlier about your question you asked me about your book. I mean, I wish you would have taught me how to do stuff, but I'm not mad about it one bit. I still love you and always will. It made me more independent and able to pick things up quickly. The most important lesson that I learned from you that I always think during life, in general, is that "patience is a virtue." Patience has made me learn things that we didn't get to experience together, but I have always looked up to you, and you are my hero. I love you, and I hope you don't feel offended.'

My conclusion is that despite me, my boys are indeed fine men. I'm very proud. Now, if I could just get them to church. I hope that my prayers will someday be answered.

One of the many key issues that my team member, i.e., Sherri and I often disagree on, is the support we give our oldest son. In my humble opinion, it surpasses encouragement and clears enablement in street shoes. The kid drives a newer vehicle than me but doesn't buy groceries or pay rent. As such, although he gets by, his healthcare is suspect, and he isn't saving much. Recall that this was the adventurous one. Meanwhile, our youngest joined the Army at Seventeen. Today he has a house of his own and a good job.

Sherri thinks that this is my chief concern. It's not. I love my kids. Despite our enabling ways, my oldest is a good man. He is constantly doing stuff that I'm no longer able to do around our place. He removes our snow in winter and mows our lawn in the summer. No, my chief concern is that both of our boys have somehow grown up with a notion that God isn't all that important, that church is optional.

"Remain in Me, as I remain in you. Just as a branch cannot bear fruit on its own unless it remains on the vine, so neither can you unless you remain in Me. I am the vine: you are the branches. Whoever remains in Me and I in him will bear much fruit, because without Me you can do nothing."—Jesus, John 15:4-5

Our inability to present a united front with respect to these matters are prime examples of ways we're failing in our marriage.

Further evidence of the chasm that lies between is Sherri's reluctance to tell you her side of this story. Moreover, she strongly opposes me telling you mine. That is why I've chosen to exclude the most important part of this chapter. Sherri is a very private person. Despite my best efforts, she has staunchly refused to allow me to include the results of my attempt to make amends. It was, in fact, fruitful and the miracle of miracles. If the Good Lord wills it, I feel safe in saying that we will make it to thirty-six years.

"Put on then, as God's chosen ones, holy and beloved, heartfelt compassion, kindness, humility, gentleness, and patience, bearing with one another and forgiving one another, if one has a grievance against another: as the Lord has forgiven you, so must you also do. And over all these put on love, that is, the bond of perfection. And let the peace of Christ control your hearts, the peace into which you were also called in one body. And be thankful. Let the word of Christ dwell in you richly, as in all wisdom you teach and admonish one another, singing psalms, hymns, and spiritual songs with gratitude in your hearts to God." Colossians 3:12-16

When Naval personnel are stationed in Japan, they're required to learn a smattering of Japanese words, chief among them is gomen or the more formal gomenasai. It's essentially an informal and formal way, respectively, to say, "I'm sorry."

During the period that I would characterize as my burgeoning spiritual awakening, a modicum of discretion may be necessary. That is because I do not wish to alienate my family any more than I've already managed. "Some make a sacrificial and heroic life their whole identity and end up making everyone else around them sacrifice so that they can be sacrificial and heroic."[67]

The final step in the Alcoholics Anonymous twelve-step program says, "Having had a spiritual awakening as the result of these Steps, we tried to carry this message to alcoholics, and to practice these principles in all our affairs."[68] In essence, a person must pass the lessons learned on to others, or there has been no gift at all. I suppose this expanded version of my original memoir, *The Gift*, is my way of finally passing these blatantly obvious lessons on. The irksome fact is that it's hard-won wisdom that came at a steep price. I suspect that I'll be repairing the damage done to my immediate family for the rest of my life. I pray that it is enough.

That said, despite Nietzsche's assertion, God is not dead.[69] In fact, he is very much alive; through the Holy Spirit. He lives in me. If anything, I'm the one who was dead. My perfidious activities wrapped me in this cloak of darkness. Only His quiet persistence has nudged me back toward the light.

Carl A. Anderson, former Supreme Knight of the Knights of Columbus, noted in a recent speech that Nietzche wrote "God is Dead" in 1882, the same year that

---

67 Richard Rohr, "*Falling Upward: A Spirituality for the Two Halves of Life*," pg. 26.

68 Hazeldon Betty Ford Foundation, "What Are the Twelve Steps of Alcoholics Anonymous?" Step 12, The set of guiding principles which outline a course of action for tackling problems including alcoholism, drug addiction and compulsion.

69 Friedrich Nietzsche, "The Parable of the Madman."

Father Michael J. McGivney founded the Knights of Columbus.[70]

After coffee with Joe, I went home and shaved. I know I have far yet to travel, and I so lament the error of my ways. Yet I'm moving forward, and I'm on "the path," I can only try to do better on the rest of my journey.

> "Brothers, I, for my part, do not consider myself to have taken possession. Just one thing: forgetting what lies behind but straining forward to what lies ahead." Phil 3:13

In retrospect, I believe that my friend—despite all "the goody-two-shoes" platitudes of this testimony—wanted me to take a moment and get real. The Trappist Monk Thomas Merton wrote, "Pride makes us artificial, and humility makes us real." This chapter was my meager attempt to "get real" and say gomenasai to Sherri and my boys.

---

70 The Knights of Columbus is the world's largest Catholic lay organization, with more than 1.8 million members around the world. The order was founded 130 years ago in 1882 by Venerable Father Michael J. McGivney at St. Mary's Church in New Haven, Connecticut. The original intent to provide welfare and security for families during times of sickness and death has grown so that last year, Knights donated more than 70 million hours of volunteer time and $158 million to charity.

Chapter Twenty-Four:

Without Wax

What does sincere mean? The definition of sincere is true or honest. Another definition of sincere is a friend who helps you without an expectation of you doing something for them in return. I am fortunate to have many sincere friends. While this is something that I'm fortunate to have in my life, I'm not entirely certain that it's a totally positive endorsement. The many kind souls that I count as friends have no expectations of repayment from me. This is something I've long sensed. My friends don't count on me for much. While that may be prudent on their part, it saddens me a bit. Most don't expect a lot out of me, except one, Joe.

Update: Recently, CBS ran a report about stem cell transplants for Multiple Sclerosis. It seems there is this cutting-edge treatment in Chicago that shows great promise. It is the same doctor and same treatment that I went out to Northwestern Hospital to evaluate more than fourteen years ago. Insurance would not touch it back then. Today, though still considered experimental, health insurers will selectively cover the procedure. What's more, the procedure is considerably cheaper than it was way back when. Initial results indicate that the medical condition of about seventy-five percent of patients on MS medication worsens over time. In contrast, that number is about fifteen percent for those who've undergone a transplant. I could not afford the program at Northwestern Hospital back in the day. The VA did it. The statistics bear out exactly what I already know. That said, there can be some significant side effects. These include sterility and death. If you live and you are done having kids, it works. I take no MS medication. At this stage of my life then, the stem cell transplant—despite costing about half a million dollars back then—has more than paid for itself in savings from medications alone.

Now, back to my story. When I was young, I had this great plan to be somebody. I remember—a day so long ago—hitting my knees to pray that my career wouldn't come to an ignominious end before it started. God answered that prayer, I believe, because He knew I was not yet "the fertile ground" where he could plant His message.

I understood—even as a lukewarm Christian—the efficacy of prayer. Yet, I never bothered to consider the long-term effects of my supplication. While I'm no longer a big enough narcissist to think that my petitions resulted in wars and other military operations that have plagued our nation over the last several years, I do regret the small role my own entreaties may have played. What I originally sought for my own glory was instead visited upon our sons and daughters, many of whom paid the ultimate price. Many more contend with life-long injuries, some of them visible. My brother-in-law did four combat tours. Our youngest son did two. His mother and I worried every single day. He is home now and out of the Army. The old me, the military officer, would sigh and lament the end of a burgeoning military career. The new me, the father of one of the young men that I love, says thanks be to God.

John Wesley wrote, "do all the good you can by all the means you can."[71] That is what the organization I belong to does. It makes my own cross seem rather inconsequential. Helping others, though my role is minimal, makes me as happy as I've ever been. "I am certain of one thing. The only ones among us who will ever be truly happy are those of us who have sought and found a way to serve."[72]

The Catholic Church is quietly the largest charitable organization on earth year in and year out. A sizable slice of that charitable giving comes from the Knights of Columbus. Drill down a fair distance, and you will eventually find the Fourth Degree Assembly to which I belong. The Knights of Columbus have a mantra "charity, unity, fraternity and patriotism." Sir Knights (fourth degrees like me) encompass, or should, all four commendable virtues. So, in addition to the many charitable things that all Knights do, fourth degrees try

---

[71] John Wesley was an English cleric and theologian who, with his brother Charles and fellow cleric founded Methodism, (i.e. the Methodist religion).

[72] Albert Schweitzer was a French Medical Missionary / Lutheran Theologian / Philosopher and 1952 Nobel Prize Winner.

to incorporate some patriotic initiatives into their giving repertoire. For instance, we lay wreaths at Christmas at the local Veterans Cemetery in my home state. This event is called "Wreaths Across America." Note: the Knights of Columbus do not exclusively run this excellent program. Veterans groups and the Veterans Administration are the major participants. In my immediate area, Fourth Degrees from all over central Iowa help lay over two thousand wreaths on every veteran's headstone in the VA Cemetery.

Knights from my assembly conceived and are executing an ambitious—albeit clandestine—plan to help veterans in my home state. It's now called the "Terrain Therapy Garden." You can check it out at https://vatherapygarden.org/ or share it with your friends on Facebook at the "Friends of the Terrain Therapy Garden" Facebook page.

One more level down, and you get to the Council where, by the time you're reading this, I used to be the Grand Knight. In that small group, we manage to touch the lives of so many all around this world.

By the way, when I refer to Therapy Garden as a clandestine plan, what I mean is that in the post-Christian society where we live, meaningful charitable gifts from any corporation are unlikely if they are tied, in any way, to religion, especially if it's Catholicism. Sad though it may be, though it originally germinated in my Council, gained its precipitous foothold in my Fourth Degree Assembly, and then gained more traction with the support of other Knights of Columbus Fourth Degree Assemblies in central Iowa, today, the VA Terrain Therapy Garden is an ostensibly secular effort. That said, I don't know of a single Knight who cares. They simply want a good thing to get done. "There is no limit to the amount of good you can do if you don't care who gets the credit."—Ronald Reagan

And so, it will. Our nation's founders said that we should have freedom of religion, but it seems that in today's world of moral relativism, many would have freedom from religion. This, then, is the battle, the war really in which we Christians must engage. Our chief weapon in the fight is love.

In Mass today, I was watching Father go through the ritual celebration of the Holy Eucharist and pondered the heavenly event taking place before me. I marveled at how this little slice of heaven coming down to earth was happening somewhere on the planet on a nearly continuous basis. Like the wave performed at a ballpark, but instead of circling the stadium, holy communion circles the planet continuously, twenty-four hours a day, seven days a week. I do not know how you feel about that, but when I'm not thinking about Jesus, it's comforting to know that someone is. Always.

I hope and pray, gentle reader, that if you are not buying what I'm selling, at least you're convinced that my story is delivered with sincerity and good intent. Long ago, I took up the hobby of writing. Back then, I was emulating great men like Sir Winston Churchill and John F. Kennedy. Essentially, I was writing to impress you and gain the esteem of a charmed public, and, ultimately, advance my own agenda.

"It was not you who chose Me, but I who chose you and appointed you to go and bear fruit that will remain, so that whatever you ask the Father in My name He may give you." —Jesus, John 15:16

What I have only recently come to understand is that my previous, and dare I say, somewhat clumsy attempts at writing were only the training ground, the boot camp, if you will, for telling you my story. I no longer write to sell books. I no longer care about garnering the admiration of my fellow man. Instead, I write to touch hearts.

The Greek word for wax is keros. In Latin, it became cera (wax). The Roman Senate once passed a law stating that all marble purchased by the government must be "sine cera" (without wax). From this law and this root comes the word sincere, which means "without deceit." I hope by now you recognize that whether I am right or whether I'm wrong, I'm telling you what I've come to believe. There is no deceit. I am without wax.

I am neither a teacher nor a philosopher. I am not some mystic guru. I am simply a man. I have no specific authority. In the parlance of my religion, I am a layperson. But I have been privileged to learn a tremendous lesson. I am a flawed individual, a pilgrim on a journey, hoping to share what I know is true.

In my original memoir, *The Gift*, I mentioned that I had been given a second chance to do something that truly mattered and how I didn't know for sure what "that something" was. That little treatise was written more than a decade ago. Now I am convinced that you, gentle reader, are about to finish "that something."

We asked for strength that we might achieve:
God made us weak that we might obey
We asked for health that we might do great things:
He gave us infirmity that we might do better things:

A Different Kind of War

We asked for riches that we might be happy:
We were given poverty that we might be wise.
We asked for power that we might have the praise of men:
We were given weakness that we might feel the need of God.
We asked for all things that we might enjoy life:
We were given life that we might enjoy all things.
We received nothing that we asked for:
But all that we had hoped for.
And our prayers were answered. We were most blessed.

A long time ago, I emulated JFK. I had started down the road of creating a rough facsimile of his life. My research was incomplete, though. When I became a Fourth Degree Knight, I discovered something I had not known about our nation's thirty-fifth president. Aside from being our nation's first Catholic President, he too was a fourth-degree Knight. I thought that I had known everything that was important to know about JFK.

Heroic, courageous, handsome, and dashing, a man of letters, tough, inspirational, faithful, but like all of us, deeply flawed, a sinner. Like all of us. Like me.

Heroic and courageous; in the early part of my life, that is the end state that I sought. Like the kid fighting for his life from his horse trailer, I eventually did become a Knight of the sky, specifically, a Black Knight.

Today, though, thanks be to the God who saved me with the gift of Multiple Sclerosis and then sent a parade of angels disguised as humans into my life. I am a Knight of a different sort. I know that opportunities to display real courage abound. Chances to be heroic happen often. The things you do or laugh at and the things you espouse publicly are an example that might lead others astray, or they can be light in a very dark world. Taking a stand for goodness and love and what is right takes tremendous courage. In this world of moral relativism, what you say, what you stand for, if it is not the norm is heroic. The war I dreamed of isn't out there on some distant horizon. It is in my home. It is in my community. It is in my workplace. It is in my heart. The world does not need one more shit hot fighter pilot. The world needs Jesus.

The End

PICTURES

My commissioning as an Ensign (E-01), September 27th, 1985

Aileron, my Golden Retriever at one year old, 1988

Me holding Nick in front of the USS Constellation.
Just back from NORPAC in 1989

Me in San Diego at NAS Miramar in 1990

Nick and Sherri watching me fly in from my first cruise in 1990

Cubi O Club NAS Cubi Point, March 1992

Cubi Flight Deck
Cubi O Club NAS Cubi Point, March 19, 1992

Cubi Flight Deck 1
Cubi O Club NAS Cubi Point, March 19, 1992

Neighbor (Patrick) with my sons, Alex and
Nick in Fallon, NV

Alex carrying a pumpkin in Fallon, NV, in 1994

Me fishing for silver salmon in Alaska in 1994

Me flying an F-5E in 1995

Me flying an F-5E in 1995

Sherri and I in front of a VFA-127 F/A–18A
Decommissioning of VFA-127

Sherri and I at an awards banquet in 1996

Older Nick holds a rainbow in the Black Hills in 2002

Me, Sherri, Nick, and Alex, Christmas 2005
in my hospital room in Seattle

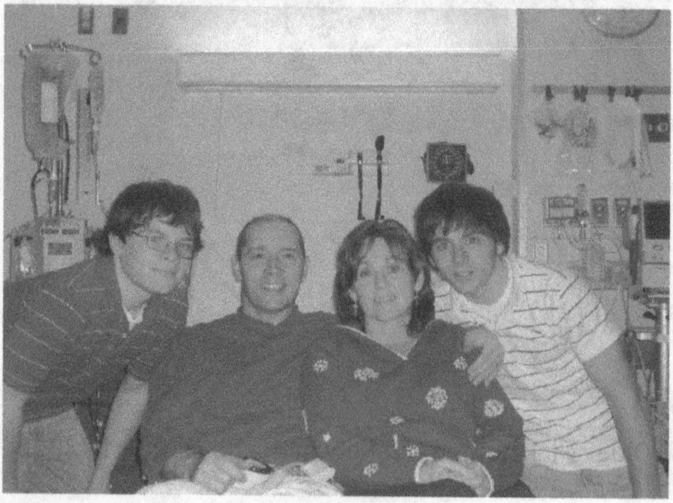

The family, with me starting to go bald

Mom and the boys, Christmas, 2005
She hadn't seen them in a few weeks.

Several of the principals running the unit are pictured here—three doctors, a dietician, a nurse, a sociologist, a psychologist, and a pharmacist.

Christmas at Grandma's, 2009

Alex, Basic Training Graduation, 2010

Nick, Sherri, Alex, and me, Fort Benning, Georgia, 2010

Target practice, 2012

Me and Sherri at a 70's costume birthday party, 2014

American Legion Post 717, 2015

Hometown Parade, 2017

Sherri and I at the Knights of Columbus
State Convention, Dubuque, Iowa, 2018

Knights manning omelet stations for Parish breakfast, 2018
That's my friend Joe with hands on hips talking to fellow Knights.

Biking with Paul, 2019

Our future daughter-in-law Erica, Alex,
me, Sherri, and Nick, 2019

Alex, me, Sherri, and Nick, Jamaica, 2019

Getting ready for the 4th-degree Knight
Ceremony at the state convention in 2019

Iowa Knights of Columbus Conference 2019

Teresa, Sherri, Carissa, me, and Carlos in 2019

Me and Sherri in Atlanta in 2019

Karl Anderson and me, 2021

Me and Dad, 2021

Addendum
2022

We live in strange times. I started A Different Kind of War in 2018, fully intending to see it published no later than 2020. So that you may realize that it was not produced in some sort of vacuum, devoid of reality, please note that because of the pandemic, publishing was delayed significantly. At the time of this addendum, the death toll from Covid-19 in the United States is rapidly approaching one million.

I do not know what the future holds, nor do I care. As I look back at the previous sentence, a quote from a John Wayne Western comes to mind, "That's bold talk for a one-eyed fat man" — Charles Portis, *True Grit*. Yet, I have decided to keep my eyes, heart, mind, and soul firmly affixed to the one who made me. I will attempt to do His will, not my own. I think that Jesus has asked me—indeed, He asks all of us at some point—to step out of the boat and, with our eyes only on Him, to "come." And when our faith may falter, He is always there to save us.

> Peter got out of the boat and began to walk on the water toward Jesus. But when he saw how strong the wind was, he became frightened; and, beginning to sink, he cried out, "Lord, save me!"

Immediately Jesus stretched out His hand and caught Peter, and said to him, "O you of little faith, why did you doubt?" Mt 14:28-31

The portion of Matthew's Gospel that I find particularly noteworthy is not Jesus walking on water. He is God, after all. It is that Peter did, at least for a few steps. It was only when he took his eyes off The Lord that he began to sink. Peter's faith falters, but what great faith he had to step outside the boat in the first place. Lord, help me to have the faith and the courage to step outside the boat. Let the wind and waves of this life not distract me from reaching You. Grant me the faith and courage to try.

About the Author

Kendall Geneser is a former naval aviator and 1993 graduate of the Naval Fighter Weapons School. Now medically retired due to a diagnosis of Multiple Sclerosis, he has cast about for a number of years, searching for meaning and purpose in his life. He has been a stock analyst, a risk analyst, and an insurance agent. In his first memoir, he has found the one thing that truly matters.

After his diagnosis in 1997, thus ending his military service, Kendall found himself a young father and husband battling mounting depression and the relentless progression of physical disability. The former Top Gun graduate was adrift in a world devoid of purpose, or so he thought. Yet, there was another way to think about the tragedy that ended his flying career.

Perhaps MS was actually a gift. It forced him to think differently. After a decade of wallowing in the morass of self-pity, Kendall was reintroduced to his Christian roots. The perceived body blow that ripped destiny from his grasp was both carrot and stick, and a life path correction delivered lovingly via God's grace.

It took a decade, but Kendall has come to the inevitable conclusion that the life he had so carefully constructed was based on his will, not His will. *Grounded* is the amalgamation of two memoirs separated by the passage of time. The author's wanderings in the desert are both a cautionary tale and an inspirational journey that likely hold a lesson or two for us all.

Kendall holds an MBA from the University of Iowa. He is the author of several works of fiction, written under the pen name of Max Cioux. He is happily married. He and his wife have two grown sons.